Joker's Wild

by

William Downes

First published in paperback by
Michael Terence Publishing in 2020
www.mtp.agency

ISBN 9781913653491

Dedicated to the memory of my Dad, James Downes MRCVS,
for pointing me in the right direction.

One

A brisk walk along the promenade, enjoying the sea air on our regular Sunday morning exercise, was the highlight of my week. We would pick up Prisha from the orphanage, and head for the seafront, with Judy spreading her whole spotty body across the back seat, with her front paws and head on my lap.

The sea was lapping at the shingle beach making a comforting sound.

The peace was suddenly broken with a piercing scream coming from a small boy sitting on the promenade wall, howling loudly. Judy had taken an ice-cream cornet out of his hand in one whole bite and swallowed it.

Judy normally followed behind us, hoovering up any dropped pieces of food, as most Dalmatians would.

I wasn't too sure what had happened, but Dad must have known, as he grabbed our hands and picked up pace.

The small child was telling his Dad what had happened to his 99 with a Flake.

"That dog took my ice cream!!" he sobbed.

"Whose dog is it?" his Dad shouted in a broad cockney accent.

Dad glanced back to observe the unfolding drama.

Saying under his breath, "Bloody pig of a dog!"

Then looked straight ahead, walking in a confident manner, as if nothing had happened.

"Hey, you!! I'm talking to you!" A loud voice came from behind.

"Hey, I'm talking to you Captain Mainwaring!!" said the same voice, but much louder.

Dad held our hands tighter and walked as quick as his little legs would go, dragging us along in his wake, ignoring the angry man.

"Keep walking, quicker if you can," Dad said softly with anticipation.

Thumping steps were coming up behind us. Suddenly they were in front of us. A large bald man with tattooed arms confronted us, pointing his fat finger into Dad's chest.

"Your dog has just ate my Son's ice cream!! What are you going to do about it??" he demanded.

"What dog?" Dad replied, trying to walk around the stocky man, dragging Prisha and Me along.

"That dog… the spotty dog. Over there!" He shouted, pointing at Judy plodding along behind us licking her lips.

"That's not my dog. I don't have a dog. What are you talking about?" Dad replied, with a stony face.

"What do you mean, not your dog?" the angry man shouted, right in Dad's face.

"I told you I haven't got a dog, so kindly leave us alone!" Dad vocalised, pushing him aside.

Judy at this point was still following without a care in the world, heading towards a family seated on a chequered blanket having a picnic.

"It's probably their dog anyway," Dad said to the confused man, pointing at the family.

We gathered pace and left the angry man to attend to his sobbing Son. Judy was pushed away from the picnickers and came running after us.

We all got in the car and drove along the seafront following the route we had just walked.

The angry man had bought his Son a replacement ice cream and saw us driving past, with Judy's gormless head sticking out the window, with her tongue flapping in the breeze.

Dad was a busy Vet, with his own practise, having very little family time. His main focus in life was caring for sick animals. As a small child of eight years old, I was used to this, and relished time with him when he had days off.

Dad was a short, stocky man, bearing a resemblance to a fatter David Niven, in looks and temperament. His pipe smoke would follow him to every room, and the smell of St Bruno would stay with me forever. He also had a wicked, dry sense of humour, seeing the funny side of life, often being outspoken resulting in upsetting people.

I would often go on house calls with him, or even sit quietly in his consulting room from the age of about ten. I enjoyed watching him attend to the sick animals. The clients would quite often hang on his every word, especially one lady who attended her appointment with her small dog, and young boy in tow.

Dad said to her, whilst peering over his gold half-moon glasses, "Your little boy is quite talented, isn't he?"

"Oh, is he? Do you think so?" she replied, glowing.

"Yes indeed," he said, looking at the young lad.

"Oh, thank you, Mr Downes," she said completely made up, smiling, knowing compliments are rare coming from him.

"Yes, in fact I have never seen a boy pick his nose and suck his thumb at the same time before, very talented," he said with a slight smirk on his face. The poor lady became suddenly deflated and couldn't wait to leave the consulting room with the little boy still picking his nose.

Memories of the Oxford and Cambridge boat race stuck with me, all cheering for Oxford to win, as Dad was born and educated there. 1966 World cup was another memorable time for me, introducing me to the English football team, which I proudly followed for many years to come. Much of my time as a small boy was to be with Dad at his surgery to help with cleaning kennels and feeding animals.

All through my life, Dad always wore the same style of clothes, a checked shirt, dark brown tie, brown trousers, dark brown leather shoes and a tweed jacket with leather elbow patches. It was like his uniform, and to finish it off, a pipe, either in his mouth or in his top shirt pocket accompanying several pens.

Posters of the World Cup heroes adorned my bedroom walls with posters of films like 'Escape to Victory' became my favourite. Dad was not particularly interested in sport, as he was more of an intellect type, reading a book, rather than participating in any type of activity that required any effort.

Over the next decade, I realised that as much as I love animals, I would not follow in Dad's footsteps as a Veterinary Surgeon, because I wasn't academic enough. I wasn't keen to study for many years as Dad was always saying that his seven years at university was a slog, and in short, I knew I wasn't as clever as him.

I was too keen to work with the public and find my own way in life. I didn't think I was in any way like my Dad, although he did his best to include me in his hobbies, particularly sailing. This was a pastime that did not interest me, as firstly, I did not have sea legs. The water motion made me quite sick, secondly, Dad's boat, a thirty-four-foot 'Westerly' called 'Gay Minstrel'.

This became an embarrassment for me. I was fed up with people shouting, "Hello, Sailor!!" echoing across the water when we were afloat.

Two

Father Joseph from Nazareth House, an avid cat lover and friend of Dad's, who also had links with a local orphanage. Father Joseph introduced him to a young Indian girl called Prisha, a few years younger than me.

Dad struck up a friendship with her and often invited her out on day trips and to help with tasks in the surgery. After a few years went by, Dad had a meeting with Father Joseph and offered to sponsor Prisha through school, college and eventually university. This was agreed with trustees of the orphanage and Prisha started her journey with Dad's kindness.

Some weekends Prisha came out with us for a 'day out', which normally included a long walk with the dogs. She really loved this special time with us, and was always sad to go back to the orphanage. Before I hit my teenage years, I was fine with this and found her good fun, but as I got older, her company became a bit irritating. She spent much time at the surgery helping and showing much interest in veterinary work. Years went by and Prisha worked her way through the education system, achieving fantastic results, enabling her to go to University to study medicine.

Life went on and I lost touch with her. Dad kept his promise to her and made sure all her educational needs were met. Prisha went to a Catholic school in Westcliff, then studied for her 'A-levels', achieving the exact grades required to get into London University.

Dad was quite rightly very proud that Prisha qualified as a Doctor and had gone to India to work in a hospital in Delhi. They kept in touch by regular letters, whereupon her adventures would be shared with all that knew her.

My academic journey was fairly dull in comparison, as my ambitions were focused in a different direction. Dad seemed proud of whatever little I managed to achieve in the academic field. His advice was, "Always be kind and honest, and leave something for someone else." These words stuck with me always.

I joined the Metropolitan Police Force, after many interviews and exams. The final interview was in front of a panel of five high ranking Police Officers, alongside three other applicants. Our task was to answer one question. "What has been your best achievement in your life so far?"

The first candidate got up and stood in front of the panel and expressed his best achievement.

"My achievement is that I climbed Mount Kilimanjaro and raised money for three different charities."

The second candidate got up and said. "My best achievement was to go to Kosovo and help build a School, alongside gaining a Duke of Edinburgh Award."

Then it was my turn. “I helped to teach disabled children to ski in Switzerland for a whole Winter season, resulting in them all being able to finish with a slalom race at the end.”

The final candidate got up and said. “I built a car out of Lego.”

The panel of five all looked at each other with dismay, as we sat there, trying not to show any emotion.

At the age of twenty-one, I started twenty weeks training at Hendon, enjoying the physical side, training with a great group of people, coming from all types of backgrounds, mostly ex-Army.

The course was demanding, especially the gruelling weekly exams. The Army guys were always working hard, sailing through the course, often helping others that were struggling, like me. They also played hard too, often pushing boundaries with the staff.

We all had to show at morning parade, dead on seven-thirty, clean-shaven, highly polished boots, and crisp clean uniform. The next forty-five minutes would consist of marching around the parade ground, being screamed at by a Drill Sergeant. He was a small ‘rat-like’ man, around sixty, rugged complexion and obviously loving every second of his job. This event would present a problem with some recruits, as learning to march takes much practice, moving arms at the same time as legs in exact unison. The Army guys were used to this, so it didn’t present a problem. I tried to follow their lead, be sure not to come unstuck and be screamed at. One recruit just couldn’t manage the co-ordination at all and became a target for the Drill Sergeant each day.

"You are like a Thalidomide octopus, don't you know your left from right?" he screamed.

These booming comments made us all laugh, trying not to be noticed. Shoulders would be going up and down, faces would be red and eyes would be watering.

"So you think it's funny to be a total spastic, do you?" he would scream.

A few that couldn't hold it together just burst into laughter, whilst trying to march in time with the rest of the group. This would be noticed, making the mouth on legs so furious, he would jump up and down in rage, screaming even more. These events often held us all to do further drills in our own time, normally six o'clock in the evening.

After twenty weeks of this, we were all as good as we were going to get. I couldn't see the point of all this, however, it became apparent that the marching was mainly for show, especially when it came to certain functions, mainly the 'passing out' parade.

The evening before our passing out parade in front of the Chief of Police, the Mayor of London, other dignitaries and our parents, was a major shoe polish alongside ironing our shirts and trousers. One helpful Army guy was giving out useful tips on how to look your very best. I was keen to learn.

I was told to turn my trousers inside out, and run soap along the creases, then turn the trousers back to normal and iron. The creases laden with soap would become rock hard. leaving very impressive razor-sharp creases. This was a good tip, I thought.

The excitement was buzzing among the twenty-six recruits on the morning of the parade. Parents were coming from all over the UK. Chairs were staged at different levels around the parade ground. A gala buffet was prepared and beautifully arranged in the large mess hall.

We were all ready to march out in our immaculate uniforms, white gloves and polished boots shining like mirrors. The first few minutes were fine, we were all in unison, even the thalidomide octopus was marching in time with the rest of the group. I could see my Dad out of the corner of my eye, desperately trying not to put a foot wrong and mess it up, not just for myself, but for my colleagues. Before we even reached the end of the first lap of the parade ground the heavens' opened. This was not just a drizzle, it was a total downpour, with rain hitting the ground so hard, it bounced back into the air.

Within seconds we were all drenched, still marching to the tune of our loud Drill Sergeant bellowing out his orders, swagger stick stuck under his arm.

Parents were huddling under brollies and coats placed over their heads.

We carried on, completing two circuits of the parade ground, as we practised so many times. All perfectly in unison with each other, white gloves swinging in time with the opposite leg. Water was pouring down my back through the gap between my neck and shirt.

I could hear distant laughter coming from the parents staged in the seating area. I looked down and saw to my horror, my trousers had turned into foam 'snow boots'. The soap had turned into an immense amount of suds, bubbling up to my crotch. I was leaving a trail of white fizzling suds behind me. We all stood at ease, in the pouring rain, luckily washing the suds away. We were dismissed and sent to the main hall. The Drill Sergeant gave me a filthy look as I walked past him. Under his breath, I heard him say, "Fucking idiot!"

My mishap seemed to brighten up everyone's day, on what turned out to be the wettest day of the year. This must have been an omen to me, as my time in the Police Force was short-lived. I realised that I wanted to spend my working life achieving more in the way of being an entrepreneur, rather than mopping up other people's crimes.

Three

A change of career in the early eighties from the Metropolitan Police led me to scan the local paper only to discover a classified advert in the job section… 'Enthusiastic person required to join a busy expanding Estate Agency'.

Within two days I attended an interview, whereupon, I met my future sales team and life-long friends. This is where the adventure started, spanning over forty years. After I just completed an intensive Police training program at Hendon, I was asked, "Do you know what hard work is?" I thought this strange coming from a lad at least four years my junior, who had no idea what hard work is himself. Over the next few months, I realised that I was correct, his name was Gary, a skilled person at 'busy doing nothing'. The other man conducting the interview, was Terry, a very smart guy, sporty and slick. He was also ambitious and a work hungry person that had a previous short career in the Police Force. Immediately we had something in common. I was asked to join the company, starting the next day. At twenty-three, I was still living at home with my Step Mum and Dad. As much as I loved animals, and decided not to work in the veterinary field. I was determined not to be a drifter, going from one meaningless job to another.

To kill time while I decided my next move, I would help Dad with evening call outs, as he did not like driving at night. I was happy to assist. My recent night visit with him was to attend a horse that had gashed its thigh on barbed wire. We arrived at a grubby smallholding at the end of a track, where the patient was in a 'Heath Robinson' style stable, barely standing.

Dad put his wellies on and followed the 'tramp like' owner into the stable to attend the cut leg. I waited in the car under instructions, quite happily listening to the radio, when suddenly Dad appeared through the decaying weatherboard wall of the stable, face first, followed by the rest of his body bouncing through the mud, thudding against a toppling water butt.

The air was blue as Dad, cursing and wiping mud from his face with his neatly pressed hanky he always had in his pocket. He got up and limped back in for round two. The horse was better behaved this time, with a tended wound, freshly stitched.

It was after this that I realised that this job would not be for me, and was pleased to have chosen to settle in as an Estate Agent. I felt sorry for Dad, after his kick up the arse, as it must have hurt. All he said on the way back, apart from don't drive too fast over bumps was that he hates horses.

The week before I was asked to drive Dad to a council estate in Southend to attend to a rather sick Alsatian. This was the third call out to this dog in a week. We both went into the house, where the owner of the dog, a large round man, with poor personal hygiene and similar wife, pointed at the poorly patient and grunted. I held the Alsatian tightly while Dad did what he had to do with this well-behaved animal. Dad fitted the cone collar of shame, and presented the dog's owner with a bill, covering all three emergency call outs. The owner said he would settle the bill tomorrow at the surgery. As we approached the veterinary ambulance (a white minivan) we noticed that all the wheels had been stolen leaving the car balancing on a pile of bricks.

Dad said, "Oh bugger, I don't believe it!"

He stropped back to the house to ask to use the phone.

"What's the problem guv'nor?" he enquired.

"Someone's nicked my wheels!" Dad replied angrily.

"Oh, that's bad luck guv'nor, I think I might be able to help though…" he said smiling.

So he made a phone call while Dad and I stood and watched. Within minutes, four wheels appeared, identical to the ones that were stolen.

"That's good," Dad said.

"It will cost you one hundred and fifty pounds guv'nor," the round smelly man demanded.

That was the exact amount Dad was charging for the veterinary work.

"Oh, I see, so basically I have been ragged," Dad said with a mixture of anger and disappointment in his voice.

The veterinary bill was torn up and we left the estate with four wheels and out of pocket. It was agreed that future appointments to this estate would be done with a member of staff waiting in the car, or insist that the patient be brought into the surgery.

The first day at the office I met the rest of the team who were roughly my age, apart from the manager, Stuart. We all came together, with different backgrounds and life experiences. After a few days we all clicked straight away and got to work with very little training, well actually, no training, apart, from being told by Stuart to look at the property details in the drawer, to get an idea of the prices in the local area.

The staff consisted of Dawn, the receptionist, Gary a negotiator, Martin a negotiator, Lindsay a negotiator, Graham a negotiator and photo developer, and Terry a senior negotiator. A mixed bag of different personalities and educational qualifications.

The company was owned by a property developer, Mr Hedges, known as 'H', an extremely successful entrepreneur, and a person I gradually looked up to and wanted to aspire to. 'H' was hardly ever seen, only contacting us by memos or the occasional phone call. It was several months before I met him and frankly, I was wondering whether he actually existed.

When I eventually met 'H', he was not what I had in mind, quite the opposite in fact. He was a slight, well-spoken man, very smart with a sun-beaten, wrinkled face. 'H' was extremely polite and respectful to all his staff, when he did eventually make a rare appearance. He told me that he knew Dad, as they belong to the same yacht club, sharing quite an interest. He politely asked me if Dad still had a boat called 'Gay Minstrel'. As he said this he had a slight grin. This caused much amusement to my colleagues.

Being keen to learn, I would want more information, so I popped into Stuart's office to seek advice. I felt that this was a fruitless exercise, as Stuart was reading one of many of his fishing magazines. His oversized desk would be scattered with sailing and fishing magazines with a central ashtray full of dog ends spilling over with ash everywhere. Stuart was not really interested and didn't seem to have a clue, although he was always friendly and sociable, offering me a rolled-up cigarette. As I was the newest member of staff, Stuart elected me to drive him to various functions, putting me in charge of his squadron-blue Jaguar. This was fine for a while as I did not mind driving, although became annoying when he was laden with alcohol.

It was a Tuesday morning, and Stuart was invited to value a superior house situated in a most desirable area. He asked me to accompany him, to perhaps learn something from him, being keen to learn I jumped at the chance. On the way there, Stuart pointed out one of the most fabulous houses in the area.

"Look, Bill, over there. That's 'Joker's Wild', one of the very best properties in this part of Essex. If we ever were fortunate enough to be instructed to sell that house, it would be a true feather in our cap!" Stuart said.

This property became a landmark for me, one day hoping to be able to see inside or even perhaps market it.

I pulled the Jag onto the long gravel drive of our destination, sweeping under a canopy of trees, leading to an impressive double fronted house, surrounded by manicured gardens. I parked in front of a quadruple garage.

"Bloody hell. This is a monster, what do you reckon this is worth?" Stuart asked.

I thought this was a strange question coming from Stuart, as he had at least twenty-five years' experience in the property business. I had no idea, suggesting that we look around firstly, then make some comparables back at the office.

Stuart insisted that we don't leave without providing a realistic valuation. We were greeted by a very well-groomed couple, who proudly guided us around this fabulous house, showing us every nook and cranny.

As the guided tour was finishing, Stuart whispered to me, "What do you think about the price?"

Well bearing in mind that I have only been in this job a few months, I had to think quickly on my feet, as Stuart was starting to panic, stuttering at the client. I knew a similar house sold in the same area with another agent recently, so I blurted out a figure.

"In today's market, this property should achieve around £550,000, however, I would suggest a marketing price of around £575,000."

I could see out of the corner of my eye that Stuart was bright red, sweating and hopping from one foot to another. There was a deadly silence, that seemed to linger for about a minute.

The clients spoke with each other out of our earshot, then eventually walked over to us and stated that our valuation was exactly the same as a rival Estate Agent. They invited us to come back and take full details in a weeks' time.

Whilst driving back to the office, Stuart implied that he was about to suggest the same price as me. I realised at this point that my future training was up to me, and not to rely on my colleagues, as their knowledge was as limited as mine. Terry was the only member of staff that seemed to have more knowledge than the rest of us put together.

The next few weeks were quite interesting as there was a formula setting in my head. The art of selling properties was about winning the instruction in the first place. After the initial marketing, properties in our area would sell themselves with very little effort, providing the price was right.

The next problem was to guide the sale through, liaising with the client, purchasers, Solicitors, Surveyors and other Estate Agents. Most of all to be patient.

I soon established that this office had its key workers who really knew the business, especially Terry. He kept himself busy and seemed to have a loyal clientele. There seemed to be a constant stream of people asking for him. I asked if I could shadow him to pick up positive tips over the next few months. He agreed, and I thought this was the best move I could have done. I learnt more in this time than I would have done working with any other member of staff in one year.

I thought that my short time in the Police Force helped me with these skills, as really I found this career much more satisfying, especially when a transaction finally goes through. The days and weeks seemed to fly by, all of us learning as we went along, making mistakes as well as gaining good results. The evenings at the office became longer, as we all tended to phone the mailing list, trying to secure appointments for viewings and valuations.

Stuart called me into his office, proudly announcing that due to my progress I could have a company car, a four-year-old Ford Fiesta popular.

This was a move in the right direction, however, the car had been trashed by the previous member of staff from the head office, who was recently dismissed. I could see that the car had never been cleaned, so my next day off, I spent hours valeting it. After much elbow grease, the car came up like new. My colleagues commented, suggesting that it was a different car.

Stuart drove 'H's old squadron-blue Jag, unless he could persuade anyone else to drive. I wondered whether this is because he did not like driving, or that he was just lazy. Stuart was rarely seen in public, which was a blessing for the company, as his appearance was not what was expected. He wore a well-used sheepskin coat, and always had a roll up in his mouth. It appeared he had a long family connection with 'H', sharing their passion for fishing and sailing. This is probably why he stayed in this employment.

Four

My colleague Martin asked me to assist him with a valuation on Canvey Island. A detached chalet situated on a larger than average plot. We were greeted by the vendor, who asked us to have a good look around then meet back in her kitchen.

Martin spoke to the owner, a middle-aged lady, about the advantages of instructing our company, then suggested an asking price.

In his next breath, he said, "Well if the property was detached the price would be about £30,000 more."

I couldn't believe what I heard, as I knew that the property was 'detached', but for some reason, Martin had it in his head that the chalet was 'semi-detached'. I decided not to interrupt him.

The lady looked quite cross and beckoned us both into the front garden, looking back at the property.

"What can you see? Take a good look, "she asked.

"Oh, I am terribly sorry, I must have overlooked that," Martin said, quite embarrassed.

The lady was furious, quite rightly too. A silly schoolboy error. Martin was very quiet on the trip back to the office, possibly with the lady's disgruntled voice ringing in his ears. She had told us that we had wasted her time and shouldn't be let loose in public. This mistake stood me in good stead for the future, making sure to check the status of the property before going inside.

The office was set out, firstly with a reception area with a couple of comfy leather settees and a coffee table laden with property magazines.

The reception desk was managed by a young lady called Dawn, who presented well, until she spoke, sporting a strong Essex twang. Behind Dawn were a row of desks, about five feet apart with negotiators, including me, sitting at each one. We were all in earshot of Dawn, sometimes having to contain our laughter when she was speaking on the phone. We would hear her say comments like, "So it's Mrs Philpott hyphen Brown, how do you spell hyphen?" You can only imagine what the client was thinking at the other end of the phone.

Dawn dropped her calculator on the floor, and muttered under her breath, "Oh bugger. I hope all the numbers haven't fallen out!" Those that heard had a chuckle.

The days went quickly, without out too many problems or dramas. Our mornings started with a pre-opening meeting, an important part of the day, setting out the plan so we all know who is doing what. During one of these meetings, Martin strolls in late, as usual, sporting a Mohican haircut. He flops into his swivel chair, sliding into the wall, scratching off more paint.

"Who cut your hair? The council?" Stuart asked, with sarcasm, and annoyance in his voice.

"What do you mean? This is fashion," Martin replied, rather surprised at Stuart's comments.

Dawn pipes up saying how cool it is, bringing a smirk to Martin's face. Gary runs his hand through the spikey mane, then complains of the grease content all over his fingers. Stuart was about to continue with a rant about Martin's appearance when there was a bang at the door. Then a series of louder bangs.

I got up to let the door banger in. The door barged open, pushing me into the window display. A disgruntled Mr Ablett came flying in clutching a dustbin bag.

"I want to see the manager NOW!" he demanded.

I looked around for Stuart, who, along with the others, disappeared into the sanctuary of his office, and the dark room, leaving Martin, Dawn and me to deal with this angry man.

"Can I help you, sir?" Dawn asked politely.

Whilst Mr Ablett was answering, he was emptying his dustbin bag all over Dawn's desk. Fragments of our 'for-sale' sign scattered across her desk and onto her lap and floor. I got up from behind the window display knocking over a large cheese plant.

Mr Ablett, an elderly man, reminded me of my old headmaster, shook the bag and shouted, "I told the chap that came round that I didn't want a board. So why was one put up? So you can have it back."

Dawn said, "Would you like a new one? We have had a delivery of a new design. I can show you if you want?"

"No, I bloody don't. I told you I don't want a board," he screeched.

Stuart was peeking through the crack in the door in his office where he was hiding, watching the escalating drama.

"Well, what have you got to say for yourself?" he said.

Martin said, "We are very sorry there must have been some sort of misunderstanding."

After a few more heated exchanges between them, Dawn offers again holding up a new design for-sale board to Mr Ablett's face.

"I just told you… NO BOARD, you cretin," he shouted to Dawn.

"What is it with you dozy morons? Firstly, you put a board up without asking me, then when I remove it and return it in pieces, you offer me another one. Then to cap it all, I have to deal with Johnny Rotten!!"

Tears were welling up in Dawn's eyes, and her face was going a nice shade of pink. She continued to scoop up her belongings that were scattered across her desk and floor. Martin walked away saying, "Silly old twat!"

I was now the only person left to deal with this angry unreasonable man. Thinking on my feet, I knew I had to defuse this situation. Pulling from the back of my head the Police training I had at Hendon, desperately trying to calm the situation down I said, "Sit down, Mr Ablett, I want to show you something."

He did, without complaint, slightly back footed. I showed him a glossy magazine that we had printed with details of his bungalow in pride of place, beautifully displayed.

He got comfortable in the leather settee and studied his details with great interest. The air was quiet while he studied every word and photo. Sniggers were coming from dark room. After a few minutes, the for-sale board had been forgotten about as his full attention was on the magazine. I offered that he could keep it, and take it home to show his family. He seemed delighted and went on his way clutching his magazine.

Stuart and the rest of the staff appeared from the sanctuary of their various hiding places, as if nothing had happened, all muttering useful comments like, "Another satisfied customer!" and, "That went well didn't it?" and, "Nice one, Johnny Rotten." Dawn expressed her dislike for this stroppy man. I then realised that most of the staff would hide from any problems. Particularly with a disgruntled client. Terry was the only one that missed the early morning excitement as he was on an appointment. Upon his return, he asked me to photograph a house he had just measured up in Hockley. Of course, I was pleased for the opportunity and jumped at the chance. Off I went in my rattling, oil leaking Fiesta to Hockley.

The vendor greeted me, a friendly lady that had obviously made a great effort to make the house extremely presentable for the photoshoot. Fresh flowers placed in prominent positions and table laid as if there was an impending dinner party.

I had the run of the house, taking photos of every room, working my way to the kitchen. Within half an hour all I had left to do was to photo the conservatory. The vendor had four of her friends sitting, chatting and sipping coffee. I asked politely if they could leave this elegant conservatory, so I could finish the inside photos. They all shuffled out into the garden, clutching their cups and saucers. After the vendor puffed up a few cushions and removed an inquisitive Labrador, I was ready to finalise the inside. This was a great success, I thought to myself.

"Just got the garden to do now, then I will leave you in peace," I said.

They all came in from the garden with the dog and left me to it. The garden was beautiful, full of flower borders, bursting with colour, with a variety of secluded seating areas under canopies of wisteria. There was plenty of choices for fabulous pictures that would enhance the brochure. I decided to walk the end of the hundred-foot garden, and take my final photo of the back of the house, showing the full width of the conservatory. The sun was in exactly the right place, so I walked backwards trying to focus the Olympus OM10 to the perfect shot, inching my way back. I felt that every move was being watched by an audience of coffee-supping ladies.

Just one more slight step back should do it, then suddenly, I was fully submerged in a 'well-like' fishpond, camouflaged with reeds and lilies. I was submerged over my head in the stinking, freezing water, with bubbles and blanket weed around ears. I was desperate not to ruin the camera, but it was too late. I couldn't believe it, as everything happened so quickly, but seemed to be in slow motion.

Stagnant water was up my nose and in my camera, it couldn't get any worse. I tried to get out, slipping back in several times in full view of five ladies, now surrounding the edge of the pond. I scrambled out, covered in mud from the sides. A dog blanket was thrown over me covered in dog hairs. This was turning into one of the most embarrassing moments of my life. My black suit was covered in Labrador hair, looking like a fur coat. Stagnant water trickled out of the camera rendering it totally useless. I really didn't know what to say, it may have been shock, although it became one of those moments where I wanted the earth to open and swallow me up.

The vendor and her friends were very respectful of my situation and ushered me back to my car using the side gate. I made my apologies and drove away as quick as I could. My thoughts were all over the place. 'Will I get the sack over this? and will I have to buy a new replacement camera?' I was also thinking that my colleagues will have a field day about this and won't let me forget it.

I decided to go home and get showered and changed before going back to the office. I threw my suit away, put a towel on the seat of the car and went back to the office. As I was parking, I could see my colleagues looking out the shop window at me, nudging each other. I hadn't realised that the vendor had rung the office explaining the disastrous morning I had swimming in the pond. The comments started with, "Nice day for a swim!" to, "Anyone fancy going snorkelling today?"

I went into Stuart's office thinking I would be sacked, however, he took it well, seeing the funny side of the escapade. The camera was also due to be replaced with a more modern digital one. He patted me on the back and said. "No harm done… keep up the good work."

I was now temporarily off the hook until my next cock-up, still being the butt of all jokes.

Five

Rumours were circulating that 'H' was about to shake the tree and clear out 'dead wood' from the company, resulting in sacking all the staff at the head office. This would be a timely shakeup as 'H' was about to release a new development of executive homes that he would need selling.

Terry was called in for a rare meeting at the head office to be told that all the staff had now gone because it came to light they were selling car batteries and sheepskin coats from the office instead of houses. Terry was asked to take over the management of the head office and choose two people to relaunch it with him. I was hoping that I would be chosen, but as I was the least experienced, didn't think I had a chance.

Terry came back to our office and announced that 'busy doing nothing' Gary had been selected to join him, He then turned to me and asked me to join as well. I was surprised at both of his choices but delighted he had asked me.

We started the next day, clearing the office completely, refreshing the paintwork and putting new desks together. It all came together quite quickly and started to look very smart especially when the new window display was installed.

Gary's skills as a boat builder in his previous job came in handy with all the carpentry jobs in the office, including putting new desks together and hanging pictures. A new secretary, Cathy, started and settled in well. We all worked very long hours to make sure the office launch was pitch perfect. The most important task was to win instructions, so we had hundreds of leaflets printed, offering a sixty per cent sole agency discount. Our next task was to walk the streets delivering these leaflets, which took a good few days and was exhausting. Within days we were inundated with appointments, some leading to instructions, which led to possible sales.

Becoming a victim of our own success in a short space of time presented problems, so we decided it might be quicker and more efficient to attend appointments together, one to do the talking, and the other to do the measuring and photos. This worked well, mostly, bringing many amusing incidents.

Two heads are better than one when it comes to appraising a property's value. A new telephone system was to be installed by a keen young chap called Shaun. He turned up at 9.30am with his toolbox and a young girl I thought may be his daughter. Stuart parked his van outside the office, freshly sign written in bold blue letters against a silver background, Shaun Hincham Information Technology, (S. H. I. T.). I offered him a coffee and asked the young girl if she would like to sit at one of the desks and do some drawing, or colouring in.

"I am Jane, Shaun's fiancé," she said abruptly. "I am here to help fit the new system, thanks anyway, but I'll pass on the colouring in."

This was yet another time I wished I could be swallowed up by the world and disappear. Then to make matters worse, Terry enquired why Shaun chose to name his company with SHIT as its initials?

"Oh, I didn't give it a thought. Yes, it doesn't look right now you have pointed it out… crap I will have to change it now," Shaun replied, deflated.

"I think that would be a good idea mate," Terry replied.

Gary and I were struggling not to burst out laughing, whilst Jane was looking daggers at us. The new system was up and running, following up with a service a month later. Shaun's van pulled up in front of the office completely re-wrapped with new signage, having changed his company name to a more appropriate name. Perhaps we did him a favour in the long run.

It was decided that there may be money to be made in financial services, so a freelance adviser called Ryan joined us and took residence in a small office at the back of the main building. Ryan was a larger than life character, loud, brash and a chain smoker. He was in his forties and still lived with his Parents, with no plans to move out. He always seemed to be in debt, which seemed strange for a financial adviser. His Mother would ring several times a day asking for 'My Ryan', to check whether he had eaten his sandwiches. It wasn't long before we all realised that Ryan would become more of a nuisance than an asset to the office. Ryan worked in a total muddle, having papers scattered across his desk and floor, as if a dustbin had been emptied over it. His ashtray would be overflowing next to at least three used coffee cups. He was such an extravert always showing off, and taking over peoples' personal space. His name plaque on his door read 'Mission Control', instead of his name. His appearance was normally scruffy, wearing the same grey suit with shiny trousers, and food splattered tie.

After complaining to 'H' about him by memo, it was decided that he stays for a six-month trial. This was met with great disappointment by the rest of us, however, we knew we had to make the best of it.

We all kept our desks and communal areas neat and tidy, so it was quite a shock to have someone in the office that didn't respect our ways. Terry had a word in Ryan's ear to smarten up and keep all areas tidy. This made no difference at all, apart from a temporary desk tidy. The weird thing is that Ryan did seem to achieve good sales figures and was popular with the younger people trying to obtain finance.

The office became a no-smoking zone, which pushed Ryan out into the car park to feed his addiction. His old yellow Nissan, we called 'the skip' would become his office. He would park in a reserved space for 'H' after always being told to keep that space clear at all times. Terry and I parked an inch from his car on both sides to prevent him from getting in, to try and teach him a lesson. This made him furious, however, he did stick to the parking policy after this.

It was Christmas time and all the staff were invited to a local Solicitor's Christmas party. We went the previous year, so knew what to expect. It was a very smart affair with a guest list extending to local MPs, the Mayor, Bank managers, and other Solicitors. We all made a special effort to look smart in our suits and well-polished shoes.

Our official invites came through the post, addressed personally to each of us, even Ryan. Gary thought it would be a good idea if we typed 'Fancy Dress' on Ryan's invite, and put it back in the envelope. We left it on his 'tip' of a desk. I had forgotten about it until the day of the party when Ryan announces that he will be attending with much excitement to the party in his fancy dress outfit. We all looked at each other, trying not to laugh. I wasn't sure if he really knew, and was just playing along with it. He mentioned several times during the day how great he will look, and kept asking what we were going as. We all replied, "It's a surprise."

I knew Ryan would thrive on the attention, and make a big exhibition out of it. The party was held in a plush hotel in Southend, Waitresses in uniforms were floating around with trays of vol au vents and trays of champagne. People were arriving in very smart attire greeted by the welcoming hosts. 'H' arrived with his wife and politely joined our little group. The party was going well, not noticing the absence of Ryan.

Suddenly the doors flew open with a bang, guests stopped talking and looked with anticipation at the drama unfolding.

Ryan skipped into the banqueting suite, shouting in his bellowing loud voice the Tarzan chant. It echoed around the room to deathly silence. Ryan stood naked in front of the Mayor and his wife, just wearing a loincloth. Everybody was dumbstruck and couldn't believe what they were seeing. Gasps soon turned to laughter as most people saw the funny side of this. The hosts ushered him out as quick as they could. Ryan was furious as he now realised that he was the butt of a practical joke, straining our future relationship with him. A memo from 'H' came through in the new year asking us to politely let Ryan go. "Get rid of that idiot."

Ryan went and kept in touch for a while, however, the experience with him, put us off finding a replacement.

Terry and I arrived at a small terraced house in Prittlewell to conduct a valuation. A small boy about nine or ten was practising his Kung Fu, kicking and thumping the air making whooshing noises and generally showing off. Suddenly without any warning, the little Ninja flew a 'roundhouse' kick to Terry's groin, lifting him into the air and piling him to the ground with a thud. He laid on the floor clutching his groin in agony. I carried on with the job in hand.

"Oh… He has never done that before," the vendor said without offering any apology. I gingerly walked past the Ninja and stepped over Terry to start measuring the rooms. About twenty minutes later, I suggested a price to the vendor, then proceeded to help Terry to his feet. Terry shuffled to the car complaining bitterly about his ordeal.

"Bloody little shitting bastard… got me right in the nuts! Not even a fucking apology," he said.

We struggled through the rest of the day with Terry walking like 'John Wayne, 'still moaning about his Kung Fu experience. Because of this I conducted all the appointments on my own, mostly without any dramas. One particular day, things seemed to be going well, until I arrived at a large Tudor-style house at the end of a long gravel drive.

The lady vendor let me in and asked me to go around the house on my own whilst she was humming to the radio in the kitchen.

I measured all the upstairs rooms and arrived at the bottom of the stairs to be greeted by the lady, red-faced and fuming. She was holding a bucket and sponge.

"You have trodden dog mess all over the house, I want it completely cleaned!!" she said angrily, handing me the bucket and sponge.

I had no idea, as I wasn't watching my feet, I was concentrating on the job in hand. It took me over an hour to scrub the carpets, regularly emptying the bucket in the outside drain, and refilling with hot water from the kitchen, with the lady scowling at me.

As I thought my day couldn't get worse, the doorbell went. It was a competitor whom I have known for a while. He walked past me whilst I was scrubbing the stairs, chuckling under his breath. My lesson that day was to take my shoes off for future valuations.

My next appointment took Terry and me to an older style house with dark beamed ceilings. I was chatting and giving the vendor advise while Terry was measuring up. The tape measure was the older type that rolls up into a leather case, with a clip on the end which attaches to a frame or radiator. Terry attached it to a Tudor-style slatting, on the wall and pulled the tape to the opposite corner to find the correct size. As he was pulling, the slatting came away from the wall, pulling down the plate rail above, with all the china plates and ornaments. The plates bounced like frisbees across the parquet wooden floor and smashing against furniture. The sound was like a tray of glass dropping from a great height. We both desperately tried to catch falling items, making the situation worse by flipping pottery vases into a glass coffee table, smashing everything they touched.

We both cursed the usual. "Oh shit," and, "Bloody hell." The vendor, an academic type was sitting in the corner of the room at a small writing table, turned to witness the carnage. He peaked over his horn-rimmed glasses, not really believing what had just happened. There was a silence for a few seconds as we were trying to scoop up the broken pieces of china. The vendor said, "I didn't expect a visit from Laurel and Hardy!"

Terry replied, "That's another fine mess I've got you into."

The vendor got up from his chair and walked towards us feeling our embarrassment, saying, "No harm done, accidents happen."

The next half an hour we cleared up all the mess and attached the beams back onto the wall. I offered to sell the house at a much-reduced commission rate to make up for the damage, pleasing the vendor and instructing us to sell. A few months later the house was sold, and on completion day, the vendor came into the office to hand over his keys. He thanked us for all our help and presented us with a photo of his sitting room with the Tudor-style slatting. "I thought you might like this, just to remind you of the beams," he said with a friendly smirk. As if we could forget.

The housing market was beginning to become busier, and we were both rushing around trying to fulfil a busy diary, whilst Gary and Cathy kept the office going.

I found myself rushing through the Saturday traffic to get to one viewing after another, trying to take short cuts wherever possible. I was running five minutes late, to show a Chinese family around a vacant house in Westcliff. This was a large immaculate house in a lovely location.

I pulled onto the driveway, noticing the family waiting, tapping their watches. 'Ok so I'm a few minutes late' I thought to myself. There were eight oriental people, Mr and Mrs Wong, four children, and two elderly parents. I opened the door and deactivated the alarms. Before I could say 'chicken chow mein', they were all in the house. Two children shot upstairs, leaving four adults wandering around opening cupboards in the kitchen, and French doors onto the garden. The other two children ran straight into the sandpit. I could hear the children jumping on the beds upstairs. Mr Wong was turning the oven on and off. Mrs Wong was trying the ice machine in the fridge, spilling water all over the floor. This was becoming a nightmare, as the owners of this house lived in Germany, trusting us to look after it, whilst showing people around.

Within ten minutes, the house was trashed by this family, with bedsheets across the floor, potpourri spilt and trodden-in over white carpets, accompanying sand and mud, dotted about the floor. The custom-made window blinds had been fiddled with and shredded out of sequence. I was experiencing total carnage and tried to herd them out as quickly as possible. At one point I really thought Jeremy Beadle was going to appear, saying. "You've been framed!"

Even on the way out, the children were pushing buttons on the alarm panel and twisting the central heating thermostat to breaking point.

At last, they were all out in the front garden, where no more damage could be done. I asked Mr Wong whether he was interested in the house.

He replied, "Oh no… We live next door, and always wanted to see inside this house, but don't want to move."

I very nearly smacked his grinning face with my clipboard. Off they went into their house next door, leaving me to inspect the damage they had caused. I desperately tried to clear up the mess in the wrecked house, however, had to employ specialist cleaners and a curtain expert to rethread the blinds. Out of courtesy I phoned the owner in Germany and explained the situation. He was very calm about it, however, instructed me not to let them back in the house again.

The following week, there was another viewing on this house which was much more successful, until we came out of the house and saw the Wong family in their garden trying to get eye contact with me. I tried to ignore them. Mr Wong walked over to me and my viewers introducing himself as the neighbour next door. He continued to say in his poor English how noisy this cul de sac is, and how the crime rate is quite high. This ruined any chance I had to sell this house to these customers. Mr Wong was turning into a pain in the arse, so I politely told him to mind his own business and let me do my job. I would never have guessed that the Wongs would play such a big part in my working life over the next fifteen years.

"Only twying to 'elp Mr Estate Agent man," he said.

In my head I was thinking, 'do I kick him or punch him?' I did neither. I rushed to my next viewing to a first floor flat in Southend, to show a young couple around. I arrived with a few seconds to spare. The young couple were already there waiting at the front door. This was the first flat on their list to view and seemed very excited. We entered the communal hallway and walked up the stairs to the first floor. All was going well. The flat was kept clean and tidy. The young couple asked lots of questions and seemed happy with the answers. I opened the door to the bedroom and they entered before me. I switched the light on and to my surprise the vendor was in bed fast asleep with his hairy arse hanging out the bed. The couple was quite taken aback, and we all quietly tiptoed out shutting the door behind us. It appeared the vendor had changed his working shifts and not told the office. The couple made an offer that was accepted and eventually moved in. During the negotiations, the buyers always referred to the vendor as Mr Hairy Arse.

I had a meeting in the office one Monday morning with one of our favourite property developers called Richard. He wanted my advice on a new hotel he was developing overlooking the seafront. This was a good instruction for us, so I was happy to give him as much time as he needed, to go through the fine details of this wonderful project. I arranged to meet his architect on-site in a week's time. About an hour passed and we shook hands and off he went.

Within a minute we heard an almighty crash. We all rushed out into the street to see Richard's brand-new BMW planted into the back of a bus.

I assumed he had not got used to driving this new car, and merely made a terrible mistake.

Luckily, nobody was hurt. I took Richard back into the office, he seemed quite shaken, and as white as a sheet.

I asked, "What happened mate?"

He replied, "Well… er … well, I um… what it was I watching a lady's bum who was walking on the pavement and the next thing I knew I was in the back of a bus!"

Later that afternoon, 'Kung Fu Kid' came in with his Mother, who was keen to view some houses. They headed towards Terry's desk, whereupon he dealt with their request. Whilst collating details from the nearby filing cabinet. 'Kung Fu Kid' was eyeing him up, possibly for round two. Terry gingerly edged back and forth to the filing cabinet, carefully covering his crotch.

There was obvious contempt for this little brat, whose Mother seemed to have very little control over.

The little brat wrapped a whole roll of Terry's Sellotape around his finger, after peeling a satsuma, leaving the peel all over the floor, whilst constantly interrupting his long-suffering Mother. His Father was outside, looking at the properties displayed in our window, totally unimpressed with the task in hand. He looked bored out of his skull, possibly dreading the thought of a property move on the horizon.

A long perusal of property details and many questions asked about schools and local amenities, the Kung Fu Kid's Dad came into the office, eating a jam doughnut, dripping jam and sugar down his chin and over the floor. He could hardly string a sentence together, let alone hold a conversation about a property move. The little brat proudly announced. "Hey Dad. That's the geezer I sparked out with a kick. Look at the size of him, and I decked him!"

The Father just grunted, showing little interest in his boy's achievement. They decided that their time in our office was too much, so they left leaving a trail of mess behind. The boy was still trying to grab his Father's attention, banging on about his small victory. Terry ushered them out shutting the door behind them, politely under his breath saying, "Fuck off and don't come back you shitbags."

I was invited to value a property in Rochford, a recommendation from 'H'. It was a detached Chalet approached by a narrow driveway, overgrown to each side with a rambling cottage style garden. The owners were Mr and Mrs Morrison, 'H's golfing partners to him and his wife, and very good friends.

It was a lovely sunny morning, an ideal day for marketing properties. I parked up on the narrow drive and squeezed out the car, stepping onto the grass. A scruffy man in well-worn overalls was rummaging around in the undergrowth happily whistling to himself. He hadn't heard my car pull up. I tried to get his attention but he was in a world of his own.

"Excuse me, sir. Is it ok to park here?" I said loudly, after a while, realising he was hard of hearing. He sort of acknowledged me with half a nod. I wrongly assumed that happy whistling soul may have been the gardener, not 'H's golfing partner.

I knocked on the door to be met by Mrs Morrison, a smart, alert lady that explained that her dream of moving is to be near the seaside, where she could entertain her Grandchildren. I listened to her, and then realised that the scruffy man in the garden was her husband.

I measured every room in the chalet and took photos as I went along. Mr Morrison came in from the garden, still in his wellies. He sat down dropping bits of garden waste over the carpet. I was told the same dreams and plans as Mrs Morrison told me in great detail. I had to repeat myself a bit as Mr Morrison was very deaf. Mrs Morrison repeated everything I said, almost shouting to get through to him.

After several cups of tea, it was time for me to go and leave the friendly couple to discuss my valuation. I squeezed back into my car and reversed out of the driveway. There was a sudden scraping sound, followed by a crashing noise coming from the back of the car. I slammed the brakes on, skidding to a stop, wondering what the hell had happened. I couldn't see anything in my mirrors. I reversed back a bit more, to find the car rocking up and down. I had driven into the gate that had been shut behind my car by Mr Morrison. The whole gate and supporting pillars, along with about fifteen feet of brick wall came clattering down, smothering the pavement with rubble and debris.

"Why had the gate been shut behind me, what am I going to do now?" I thought.

Mrs Morrison came rushing out of the house to see what all the commotion was about, followed by her husband. Neighbours also appeared to investigate.

I got out of my car to discover the extent of the damage I had caused. Everything seemed to be in slow motion, seeing mouths moving, but not hearing anyone. All sorts of forthcoming problems were spinning in my mind. Of all the people to upset and damage their property, would have to be the Morrisons. My boss's good friends.

Mr and Mrs Morrison were standing in front of me scanning the damage. I really thought that they are going to be furious and 'H' would give me the sack.

To my surprise and relief, they both apologised to me, as Mr Morrison owned up to shutting the gate behind me when I arrived. The gate was a small metal framed gate, standing only two feet tall, hardly visible from the car whilst reversing and not really worth bothering with, as people could just step over it. Not me, I just drive over it.

I helped clear some bricks off the pavement and offered to pay for repairs.

Mr Morrison said, "No. No. We won't even think of it. It was entirely my fault." As he was talking, Mrs Morrison was moaning at him for shutting the gate behind me. An Army of neighbours had the carnage cleared with minutes. I drove back to the office and told my colleagues of my plight, which was, as expected met with a wall of laughter.

I decided to come clean and tell 'H'. So I rang him at home. Nobody ever rings him, disturbing his peace at home. Mrs 'H' picked up the phone.

I politely asked to speak to Mr Hedges.

"Yes boy. What's the matter?" he asked.

I replied, expecting a bollocking, "I thought I should let you know that I went to value your friend's house, Mr and Mrs Morrison earlier today and had a slight accident."

'H' Said. "I'll stop you there, lad, I know what happened as I have just spoken to Philip Morrison and he has put me fully in the picture."

My hands were sweating with anticipation of my fate.

'H' carried on talking to me. "I don't know why he has a thing about shutting his gate. A strange habit, I suppose. Don't worry lad accidents happen. I appreciate the phone call though. I am sending one of my builders round on Monday to fix it, so no harm done."

I was so relieved and explained that the car had no damage. This debacle broke the ice between us, whenever he made a rare appearance at the office, he always said, "Backed into any gates recently, lad?"

The internet was beginning to play a major part in property sales, and being part of a large prominent web site became an important marketing tool. More agents were working in competition with us, setting up within a quarter of a mile of our office, and offering much-reduced fees. This healthy competition kept us on our toes, although we had to become less picky who we dealt with, which brought some interesting characters.

We coped with this for many months, eventually, with clients coming back to us, as they did not get the service they were expecting with rival agents. Some clients still wanted our attention all the time, not wanting to believe we had other clients to deal with as well. Some people could be very rude, unnecessarily, kicking off with abuse and sometimes violence.

As humans, offering a professional service, we found this not acceptable, and when we came face to face with an arse, we ushered them out of the office as soon as possible.

One morning, we all sat quietly at our desks, happily doing paperwork and filing. A small man burst in through the door shouting "Bungalows!" None of us even looked at him. We just carried on as if nothing had happened, ignoring this ignorant cretin.

"I said Bungalows!" He shouted again.

He was now becoming impatient, so he walked over to Terry's desk, putting his Gorilla like hands on it, whilst leaning forward with his head level with Terrys.

"Bungalows… got any Bungalows?" he blasted.

Terry looked up uninterested and said softly, "I suggest you walk out of this office, and come back in again with some manners, asking politely what you require."

The angry man reeled back in surprise at Terry's comment and answered. "Don't you want my business then?"

"Not really," Terry replied.

"I have never heard anything like it in my life… Call yourself an Estate Agent, you arsehole?" he shouted, spaying Terry with spit.

Lulu stood up, and slowly walked across to the animated angry man, who was now hopping from one leg to another and said calmly, "Pop along, sir, and don't come back."

The chap, with small man syndrome, went off complaining and shouting to the safety of the pavement. It is not worth dealing with people like that. We have many years of working life ahead of us, so why waste it on idiots who will never change and be polite. This working strategy held us all in good stead over many years ahead.

Some people may be a little different or have strange ways about them. Although they don't look how you expect, they are normally very polite and respectful. One person was keen to view flats in our area, over the next two weeks, while He or She was on annual leave. The reason I mentioned He or She is because this person was completely sexless. There was no clue to whether this person was Male or Female. The only resemblance to any male would be the Child Catcher in Chitty Chitty Bang Bang. The name was Professor Harding, so no clue there either. The looks were very plain, slight build, unisex clothes, unisex sensible shoes, unisex glasses and greasy bowl-cut hairstyle. Professor Harding spoke in a soft articulate voice, claiming to be an academic, attending lectures at Universities across the UK.

I researched the name and discovered that the first name is Sam, who had written many books on scientific subjects. Sam is a name that could be any sex, so still no clue. Professor Harding was a pleasure to deal with, especially when a suitable property was found. I was asked to meet again at the favoured property to measure up with a partner, prior to moving in.

I met them on a Sunday, as they had a busy working week in another county. I thought that by meeting the partner, might give some clues about Professor Harding. We met at the property, and I was introduced to the partner as Doctor Clarke.

Unbelievably, Doctor Clarke looked almost the same as Professor Harding, only slightly larger. They both wore the same style of clothes and had identical greasy haircuts. During the viewing Doctor Clarke was called Lee by her partner a couple of times. They moved in a month later, bringing me a bottle of wine as a gift, when they came to the office to collect their keys.

To this day, the mystery of the strange couple has stayed with me.

Six

A welcome phone call from my Dad came at a time that my week had been very stressful.

"Do you fancy a four-day trip to France with me?" he asked.

"Yes, that would be great, when are you thinking of going?" I replied.

"Monday, first thing. I have bought a boat from Edmond, and I thought we could go out to see him and his family, have a bit of chill time, then tow it back," he replied.

Edmond is a life-long friend of Dad's and also a Vet. His son Eric came to stay on a French exchange in his teens, and I went to a return stay there one Summer.

I was pleased to be asked, as I hadn't seen this family for at least fifteen years. Really, Dad wanted me to do the driving, as he was not cut out to drive on the wrong side of the road, as we found out once in Majorca, ending up in a ditch.

We left in good time in his almost new Granada, arriving at the Port of Dover to board the Ferry.

A smooth crossing to Calais, and we were off, following the scenic route. The car was a dream to drive, as we made progress through quaint Villages and Towns, stopping for regular stops for refreshments.

We arrived at St Michel en l'Erm, not far from La Rochelle, to a warm welcome from our hosts. A barbeque meal was cooking nicely and plenty of cold beers were on offer. The hosts' chateaux, was as I remember, very large, with numerous outbuildings, converted into comfortable accommodation. An immense lawned garden leading to a lake, stocked with a variety of fish. A good night's sleep, followed by a large mug of hot chocolate accompanied by warm croissants for breakfast was most inviting.

We followed Edmond, a large man with as much hair as an Ape, to a small harbour in La Rochelle. The boat was waiting for us, sitting awkwardly on a rusty trailer. I noticed the name plaque, 'Jambo', a vast improvement on 'Gay Minstrel'. The rather scruffy, clinker-built vessel, was a fourteen-foot 'Tideway', desperately needing a new home. Edmond explained, in his poor English that the boat belongs to his Son, and now he has moved out, he rarely has time to sail it.

I thought it was a Lemon of a boat, however, Dad was over the moon with it, and couldn't wait to sail it. I pushed and wriggled with it until it sat properly on the trailer. After pumping up the tyres with a nearly useless pump, I strapped it on securely. All of Edmond's family met at the harbour with us and suggested we had lunch at one of the harbour bistros.

The drive was much slower on the return journey, due to the weight of our cargo swaying around behind us. We decided to stay in a friend's apartment in Calure, breaking up the journey. Dad had stayed there before and quite rightly said it was one of the nicest towns he had stayed in.

The problem was soon apparent that the trailer was quite wide, not the best transport for these narrow roads. Parking became impossible, so I pulled into a small car park adjacent to the town's supermarket, directly opposite the apartment, with the intention of leaving it there overnight.

Whilst I rejigged the boat and trailer, tightening the awning and straps to make it safe, Dad went into the supermarket to ask permission to leave our car and boat there overnight. This would be ideal because we could see the car out of the apartment window.

Dad loves these types of shops, particularly if they sell wines and cheese. I knew he would be in there a long time.

"Ah Monsieur, pardon me," Dad asked, to get the owner's attention. A small bearded man with a red jolly face, popped out from behind the glass counter, displaying many varieties of cheeses.

"Qui Monsieur," he replied.

"Je suis un Bateaux!" Dad said, whilst pointing out of the shop window at the boat, not realising that he had just introduced himself as 'a boat'.

With a bit of pidgin English and miming, the jolly shop keeper kindly agreed to Dad's request.

At this stage, I had no idea that Dad had introduced himself as a boat, it was only when we went back to get some groceries for the evening, the jolly chap shouted in a friendly laughing voice. "Aww. Monsieur Capitain!!"

They chatted and laughed a while. I went back to the apartment to freshen up and prepare a meal for the evening, Dad was still in the supermarket chatting away to his new friend. He eventually appeared, slightly half cut. They had been tasting wines.

The next morning we set off after handshakes and goodbyes with Dad's new friend. We were presented with a large strange coloured cheese, which stank the car out all the way home. For some reason, Dad didn't want to put it in the boat.

The trailer seemed to be towing a heavier load, for some reason, and listing to one side too. I stopped several times to tighten the ratchet straps and happy with the load we carried on.

I pulled onto the Ferry at Calais, trying to negotiate a large awkward load into the smallest space you can imagine. I drove off the ferry and headed towards the custom control area following the green arrows to the 'nothing to declare' lane. We queued patiently, edging towards the exit.

A few more metres at snail's pace speed, we were beckoned to a hatched area with five customs officers waiting for us. It seemed that they were stopping every fourth vehicle for a thorough inspection.

We were told to get out of the car and wait in a small office overlooking the custom workers pulling our belongings out of the car and boat. Our belongings were thrown and scattered across the ground with Alsatian dogs sniffing all over it. Even the cheese got a good slobbery sniff. Bags were opened and emptied onto the ground, with clothes spread across tables.

At this stage, I wasn't concerned, as I knew we were in the correct 'nothing to declare' area. The buoyancy bags were pulled out from under the seats in the boat and flung to one side. To my horror, I saw bottle after bottle of wine appearing and placed onto a table by smirking officers. A female officer was writing everything down in great detail. Dad looked a bit sheepish as it was coming to light that he had obviously done a deal with his shopkeeper friend in Calure. So Mondieur Capitain had stocked up with over sixty bottles of French wine and hid it in the boat. No wonder the cargo seemed heavier and we were presented with a cheese!

I was lost for words, thinking we are in so much shit. We were taken into an interview room, whilst the car and boat were roughly put back together. The bollocking to both of us went on for about half an hour. Dad explained that I didn't know about the wine, and eventually was allowed to go back to the car. Whilst Dad was having the riot act read to him, I was repacking the boat and strapping securely onto the trailer. A little while later, Dad appeared looking pissed off and angry. He got into the car clutching the paperwork that he was given.

"A three-hundred pound fine and all the wine confiscated!!" he cursed. Shame they didn't take the cheese, I thought.

We pulled out of the docks with a much lighter load with Dad still miserating about his ordeal.

"Bloody customs officer, flapping his hair lip at me for forty-five minutes, then taking all my wine, the robbing shit!" he ranted.

We decided to keep this to ourselves, as poor old Dad would have been hauled over the coals again if my Step Mum heard about it.

A few years later, Dad went back to La Rochelle with some of his friends and stopped off at the small supermarket on the way, being greeted with, "Aww Monsieur Capitain!"

He didn't buy any more wine. So he says!

I was pleased to get back to work, although enjoyed my time away.

Terry and I went to Richard's Hotel conversion on the seafront to meet his architect, Clive Grey, to discuss the division of communal areas and specification to the finished apartments.

We arrived at the site, to a tower of scaffolding, and hive of activity, with builders coming in and out with wheelbarrows and planks of wood. The site foreman found us and told us to put on the hard hats and wait in one of the rooms near the front door.

After a few minutes, we heard the clacking of high heels coming along the wooden floor. A little old lady appeared in a flowing bohemian dress and floppy cardigan. She had bubbly ginger hair with a pink beret on top and looked at us through her diamante glasses. A wicker shopping basket was placed over one arm, the other arm was extended with her hand in a white glove to shake hands with me.

"Can I help you, dear?" I asked.

"No, But I can help you," she replied.

I was quite confused, as I was expecting to meet Clive.

"I'm Claire Grey, Richard's architect," she stated.

"Oh… er … I was expecting to meet Clive Grey," I said, still confused. Terry was grinning from ear to ear. Builders were stopping what they were doing and watching with interest the cabaret evolving in front of them.

The little lady bent towards me placing her chin on my shoulder with one hand on my arm, and whispered in my ear.

"I am Clive, but today I am Claire."

"Oh… I see. Nice to meet you, Claire. I am Bill and this is Terry," I said, realising the situation.

I could hear sniggers coming from builders, and could sense them nudging each other.

We got on very well, going through 'blueprints' and making decisions that will enhance the development.

Over the next few years, Claire was a regular visitor to our office, as she was instructed by many developers to design their projects. She even did the plans for an extension on my house.

There were changes happening in the office, Cathy decided to leave, so we started interviewing for a replacement. We employed a typist called Mary and an office junior, Carly, both settled in quite well, although both had different personalities and seemed to want to work on their own, not as a team.

Carly was only seventeen, a tall young lady that moved around the office like a sloth, without any urgency or purpose, however, she was keen to learn, even though Mary set her up with the most minimal of tasks. Mary assumed charge as she was older and more experienced.

By this time, I was working long hours to support a young family. The property market was in a recession, so all sales were important, becoming more difficult to construct and to keep together.

I pleased to sell a large extended house in Maplin Way, Thorpe Bay, for Mr and Mrs Clayton. This started as a nightmare negotiation, selling to a delightful Indian couple, Mr and Mrs Nawaz, who put up with much chopping and changing from the Claytons.

Mr Clayton was a large imposing man with the stance and appearance of an Army General, complete with a handlebar moustache, and clipped upper-class accent. He was keen to sell quickly, and within days of introducing the buyers, involved in a long chain, my work began. Mr Clayton was on the phone to me three times a day minimum. Hours of phone calls, up and down the chain, to establish details, leading to a much-anticipated exchange of contracts. Mr Clayton had treated me like a magician as if I could magic a completion day out of a hat.

Eventually, the Claytons moved out and the Nawazs moved in. The next day was a Saturday. Mr Nawaz contacted me at the office, upset that the Clayton's had taken items that should have been included in the price. These items included a washing machine, dishwasher, an American style Fridge Freezer and all the light fittings, even the light bulbs.

I expressed my sorrow, promising to look into it. I tried to ring Mr Clayton on the only number I had, which was his mobile, unfortunately, without success. I phoned Mr Clayton's Solicitor first thing on Monday and told him of his client's behaviour. The Solicitor was extremely helpful, however, knew nothing about his client taking out items that should have been left. Also, he stated, that he had not been instructed to pay our fees of around eight thousand pounds, that Mr Clayton will pay them direct. To make matters worse, the Solicitor didn't have a forwarding address for his client as they were moving in with family, supposedly. A client owing this amount of money, and stripping the house of items that were contractually meant to be staying, rang alarm bells with me. I realised that the Claytons could have moved anywhere, or even abroad never to be seen again.

I decided to make enquiries with the neighbours, all of which implied that they were glad to see the back of him. My Dad used to say to me that some people in this area are 'all bowler hats and no breakfast'. I was beginning to learn this for myself.

A few years later, on my day off, shopping in Tesco's with my wife and children, just doing normal grocery shopping and edging my way to the checkout, I heard a familiar clipped military voice coming from the front of the queue. I looked and saw Mr Clayton, as bold as brass twiddling his moustache, watching his wife pack the groceries into their forever hessian bags. It was exactly as I remembered him, loud, larger than life and wearing the same clothes. All sorts of thoughts came into my head.

"Do I confront him now and possibly cause a scene? Do I ignore him?"

My Police training kicked in. I decided to remain conspicuous, blending into the background. I whispered to my wife and asked her to continue with the checkout while I follow him. I couldn't believe my luck. What are the chances of bumping into this guy in Tesco's? I followed the con artist to his car, and memorised his registration number. I really wanted to confront him and tell him what I thought of him, but decided to follow a legal route. I phoned a mate of mine who was a Police Sergeant and told him of my problem. He managed to find the Clayton's address by tracing the car registration number.

The next day, I contacted my Solicitor giving all the information and details to prepare a writ. I picked up a writ, freshly prepared, and drove to the address that the car was registered to. Pulling up outside, the car was on the drive. I rang the doorbell a couple of times, until Mr Clayton appearing not to recognise me.

"Yes. What do you want?" he asked in a curt voice.

I replied, handing him the writ. "I have a writ for you, for an unpaid commission for selling your house."

He looked stunned, that he had been caught out. There was a silence for about thirty seconds.

"I thought my Solicitor paid your account," he said.

"You know full well that you had no intention of paying. And also you took loads of items that were included in the price. I will give Mr Nawaz your address, so he may take it up with you directly," I said with force.

Mr Clayton was fuming that he had been caught out. Walking towards me and shutting the front door behind him, he muttered.

"Ok, I will give you a cheque!"

With that comment, he opened the boot of his car and pulled out his briefcase. I watched as he stumbled for his chequebook and reluctantly wrote a cheque for the full amount. He didn't say anything else to me, just threw his briefcase back into his car and sloped off into his house banging the front door behind him.

I was pleased to let Mr Nawaz know of the Clayton's new address.

At the office, there was the usual number of messages and phone calls to make. I had been dealing with a purchaser called Gordon Parker, who was born deaf and only spoke face to face. It was getting near to completion on a flat he was in the process of buying, so he was wanting a meeting to discuss possible moving dates. He was a likeable, friendly chap, deep down I admired him for making a normal life in the community and generally getting on with it. For some reason I was the only member of staff that could understand him, I really think that I was probably the most patient at that time. He went away quite happy, and in a month or so he moved into his new flat. Gary was attracting much attention from young ladies, and loving every minute of it. He decided to have a shaggy perm, which I suppose was the style in the 1980s and he was right on-trend.

We all had to increase the sales, mainly because 'H' had changed the commission structure, benefiting all the staff, falling in line with the first phase of his luxury housing development. At this time we decided to take potential buyers out in our cars to view properties when appropriate. This worked well, however, did attract some time wasters and sightseers.

Gary started going out with a girl who worked in the accountants directly opposite our agency, on the first floor, enjoying views right into our office. She was called Angela, we soon labelled her 'Little Miss Angela'. (LMA). She appeared to know Gary's every move, as if she had a telescope trained on him.

There was a film around at this time called 'Fatal Attraction' and 'Bunny Boiler', came to mind. At first, Gary could not see that his moves were being closely monitored, as the old saying goes, 'love is blind'. It was only when Gary took clients out in his car that she would kick off. Gary's client called Tallulah Beckett, a young attractive lady, working as an air hostess at Stansted Airport.

Miss Beckett made regular visits to our office, particularly wanting Gary's attention, and for him to show her around many properties. She was always heavily made up and tottered around in high heels and short skirts. Gary was loving it, telling by the excitement of her impending appointments, and the smile on his face when she arrived for her afternoon out.

He had obviously told LMA about this client, however, she stormed into the office after Gary drove off with Miss Beckett. "Where's he gone with that tart?" she screeched.

Cathy replied politely, "He has gone on some appointments, and won't be back for a while."

"I saw him driving off with that 'Toilet Bucket' all dolled up to the nines," she replied, angrily, storming out of the office.

After a few hours, Gary returned and his client went away, after making further appointments for the following week. Cathy told him that LMA had been kicking up a fuss. As she was explaining to Gary, LMA was crossing the road on route to the office.

Gary shot outside to confront her, opening the boot of his car, pretending to look for something. After a short burst of a screaming tantrum, she slapped him across his face so hard he recoiled into the boot.

Gary shuffled himself out, as she marched across the road shouting obscenities at him. He fiddled around for a while as if to say 'nothing to see here!' Eventually, he came back into the office sporting a red cheek and slid quietly into his chair looking very embarrassed.

Over the last few weeks, Gary had been leaving chocolate bars under LMA's windscreen wipers on her car she parked in the next road. Of course, we found out about this, and one of us, normally me, would remove the chocolate and put the wrapper back. It was only when she mentioned it in the office that 'bloody kids' keep leaving rubbish under my wipers, Gary realised and stopped.

They eventually split up, although we were all sure that our every move was being watched. Miss Beckett parked outside the office to see Gary. As she tottered up to our door, fully made up, and with an even shorter skirt, squinting through the window display as she got nearer, trying to catch a glimpse of Gary, she stumbled headfirst into the glass door, sinking slowly to the ground, leaving a pinky, orange makeup stain. She got up, straightened her attire, and tottered away, never to be seen again.

Every morning I was normally first in, so my routine was to switch on the computers, listen to the answerphone messages and put the 'open sign' out.

Most mornings I would see Kevin being dragged past with Scooby, a wonderful Great Dane. I wondered if Kevin had one arm longer than the other. He would always try and stop to say hello, however, Scooby had other ideas. Sometimes Kevin would fall and become dragged along for a while until he managed to clamber back onto his feet.

I always wondered why people had pets that completely controlled their lives, but Dad used to say that English people are 'nuts' about their pets, possibly treating them better than their own children.

Dad's old friend, Father Joseph often walked past the office, normally looking in to see if I was busy, so he could come in for a chat. If I was caught 'off guard' he would come in and sit in front of me for at least half an hour, telling me about his life in great detail. My mind would go blank, focusing on his teeth sticking out in all directions, in various shades of brown. I was always polite and respectful, because he goes back a long way with my Dad, both raising money for charities, mainly guide dogs for the blind. Also, he would recommend our company to his parishioners who were planning to move house, in fact, over the years, we had moved at least four families that were connected to the parish.

For more than thirty years, Dad looked after many cats kept by an eccentric lady called Miss Brenda Day, who lived as a recluse in a large house that she shared with her sister who sadly passed away many years ago. The only person she let into her house was Dad, to treat her cats, sometimes with me in tow.

I found over the years that these visits were fascinating, as the house hadn't been touched for years, at least since her sister's passing. There were cobwebs everywhere, wallpaper peeling off with damp, and heaps of rubbish piled up high in every room. The kitchen was full of empty cat food cans, with flies circling around like fighter planes. The tree growing through the dining room window got more mature over the years, letting in rain, causing terrible damp problems. The house was similar to Miss Faversham's house in the film 'Great Expectations'.

Miss Day, a slight, grey-haired lady, possibly in her fifties, however, looked in her eighties, lived on nuts and pulses, always stinking of garlic. There was even a box of half-eaten 'Lucky Strike' chocolates rotting away on the sideboard, next to a faded photo of her sister.

Miss Day was one of Dad's charity cases that he picked up along his journey as a Vet, never charging her for his services, attending to her twenty-plus cats. Even in my teenage years, I would take the homemade soup that my Stepmum made especially for her. She would hear my moped pull up outside, and open a window upstairs to make herself known.

"I have your soup for you, Miss Day," I would shout.

A frail voice would answer, giving me instructions to put the thermos into the basket that she lowered down from the window, on a tatty rope. I put the goods in the basket, then she hauled it up, took the soup and lowered the basket back down with yesterday's empty thermos in it. I was clear that she lived in one small room at the front of the house. She would shout, softly. "Thank you for the doup."

Because she had lost her teeth, it was difficult for her to pronounce 'S's, they always sounded like 'D's. Normally my Stepmum would do this daily task, however, I was happy to help when she was unable to do it.

Many years later, Dad couldn't get her attention to door knocking or shouting up at the window. Eventually, he got in through a broken door at the back of the house, finding her in the sanctuary of her bedroom with all her cats around her.

She passed away peacefully in her sleep. All the cats were rehomed. Some months went past, when Dad announced that he had inherited the house of his reclusive friend, asking for my help to clear it, and eventually sell it. The house sold, and all proceeds went to the 'Guide Dogs for the Blind'.

This was very ironic, as Dad went blind after he retired, having a succession of Labrador guide dogs.

Seven

We battled through the recession hoping to come out the other side without too much debt. Carly announced that she had arranged for Mr Moore to be picked up and taken to three properties this afternoon. She asked who would like the honours?

Gary, 'busy doing nothing' looked down pretending to be busy writing on his diary. Terry was genuinely busy, so, I was happy to take the appointment.

All the viewing times had been carefully arranged at regular intervals, sensibly adding travelling time between each one. It was half term, so all the vendors were in to let me bring the applicant along to view.

I left the office in good time to meet Mr Moore at the agreed rendezvous address. Mr Moore was waiting and climbed into my car. He was very polite and introduced himself as 'Bobby'.

I realised he was Bobby Moore, the football legend, and was dumbstruck for a few seconds.

"I am pleased to meet you. I am Bill," I said, determined not to mention football, and be professional.

Mr Moore then said. "Thank you for driving me around. I'm not too sure of the area yet. I am starting as Chairman of Southend United in a month's time, so I need somewhere to live."

I replied, "I am pleased to help you. It's a pleasure."

Whilst driving to the first appointment, I was thinking back to 1966, watching the world cup final with my Dad.

The next three hours, football wasn't mentioned, I didn't even let on that I recognised him. We spoke of properties, events and other interests around the Southend area. I couldn't help thinking that when I was a child I had a poster of the 1966 English football team on my bedroom wall, and now I am in the company of this humble hero.

During the viewings, I introduced Bobby as Mr Moore to my clients as he followed me into their houses. The first vendor had no idea who he was at all and left me to conduct the viewing. The next two houses, the vendors knew who he was and could not believe that Bobby Moore was looking around their houses. They were amazed and stared awkwardly, offering cups of tea. Bobby declined and kept the viewings to a more formal format. We finished the viewings, unfortunately, as each property was either too small or in the wrong location.

I was not thinking that this was a waste of time, as this was one of the most memorable times of my life. I arrived back at the office after dropping Bobby back to Southend football ground and told the staff of my adventure with a football legend. Terry then said that he had heard Bobby Moore was joining Southend as Chairman, and wished he had volunteered to do the appointment. They all wanted to know in great detail of my day out.

We were unsuccessful in finding him a house, however, he kept in touch, ringing me and asking advice on other properties. I was only too happy to help.

A few months later, I was attending a function with my Dad and his partners at a plush hotel whereupon Bobby Moore was a guest alongside shareholders of Southend football club. I walked into a crowded reception with Dad and his guests. Dad's senior partner was an avid football fan and a season ticket holder at Southend.

I heard, "Bill… over here!"

I couldn't see who was calling me. My Dad said. "Someone's calling you… the chap over there."

Bobby Moore came over to me and I introduced him to Dad and his partners, who were amazed. He had a drink and chat with us, and continued to mingle. Dad didn't have a clue who he was, but his partners said that they will dine out on this for years.

Gary decided to leave to pastures new, planning to follow a different career. Although he was generally lazy, we all missed his company, as he is a funny character. 'H' decided to retire and gave Terry the opportunity to take over the ownership of the company, which in tandem gave me the chance to become self-employed, working on a commission-only basis. There was a gap that needed filling, so after a few interviews, a young chap called Lucas joined our team. Lucas knew the business as he was working for a rival company. Lucas was a huge man in his early twenties, well over six-foot-tall and built like a sumo wrestler complete with shaved head.

Although Lucas looked intimidating, he was a gentle giant, being very popular with the younger clientele, frequenting the local bars and night clubs. This type of networking was extremely successful in finding new clients.

Terry and I decided to become fellow members of the National Association of Estate Agents, which we knew would lift the professional status of the company, as we were not getting any younger. Over the years, we were glad we did. The new team prospered in a rising market. Lucas was happy to do any task, no matter how difficult or mundane, becoming affectionately known as 'Lulu'.

I was invited to value a house in Westcliff, a Tudor-style former rectory. I arrived and offered to take my shoes off. The vendor, Mrs Snoad, was happy for me not to, as some of the rooms were in the process of being decorated. I started measuring the rooms and photographing the downstairs while the vendor was in the kitchen, clattering about with pots and pans.

The small snarly 'Jack Russell' followed me around, watching my every move, generally getting under my feet, and making it difficult for me to take photos without him being in them. Just as I was getting the camera into focus, I felt a sharp nip on the back of my heel. I had been bitten by this bloody dog. I pushed it away with my foot with it still snarling at me. Although feeling uncomfortable, I carried on to the first floor with the aggressive dog right behind me. Failed attempts to entice it away, without Mrs Snoad being alerted, were beginning to get on my nerves. I felt my shoe filling up with blood, I bent down to pull my sock away exposing a nasty wound, gaping with a jagged hole, seeping blood.

I began to feel a bit wobbly, seeing black dots in front of my eyes. I am still baffled why I didn't faint. Eventually, I descended to the ground floor, leaving dots of blood on the carpet. The snarling dog was still trying to bite me, going for my other leg. I was having none of it and kicked it full-on in its face, catapulting it away from its target. The yelping creature rapidly slid on its backside, across a highly polished wooden floor, smashing into a raised brick fire hearth. It flopped down with its legs in the air for a while, stunned, then suddenly got up, and shook itself down, and ran into another room. By this time my shoe was full of blood, and I knew that this would be a hospital trip for me.

"What the hell do you think you are doing? How dare you kick my dog!!" screamed Mrs Snoad.

I hadn't realised that she witnessed the whole incident.

"Well, it bit me, and tried to bite me again. Can't you control this vicious thing?" I replied.

I edged my way out through the front door with Mrs Snoad screaming in my face.

I could see the fillings in her teeth and whiskers on her chin. I felt her spit on my chin, and my ears ringing as she was inches from my face. She snatched my clipboard out of my hand and threw it into a tree, with the strength of a shot putter. I left it up there and limped into the sanctuary of my car, with Mrs Snoad banging on my roof, still cursing and screaming so loud, neighbours were appearing to witness the scene.

After four hours waiting in A and E, I was eventually stitched up and given a tetanus injection. Unsurprisingly, the house never came onto the market with us. Strangely I noticed the clipboard still wedged in the tree several months after this incident.

I was reported to the Police for kicking her dog, luckily after mentioning it to my Dad, he confirmed that the dog had a history of biting people and even bit one of his Veterinary nurses recently. The case was dropped against me.

We all tried to leave the office by six-thirty otherwise we would be caught by our trusted cleaner, 'my Ben Lynn'. She was a bubbly middle-aged woman, whose life surrounded her only son, Ben. Nearly every sentence she spoke, Ben would be mentioned.

"My Ben is such a good lad!"

"My Ben goes to the gym. Every day he is getting more like Arnold Schwarzenegger!"

"My Ben and his partner Alex are such a lovely couple!" And so on.

During her many years cleaning the office, we never saw Ben, or even a photo. I often wondered if Ben actually existed. Of course, he did exist, and his exploits were shared in great detail when there was a willing audience. Lynn appeared at 6.30pm, and I was still working. My heart sank, as I then knew I would be caught for a long chat by her.

An hour later, I was still edging towards the door for my escape. Ben was mentioned thirty times. How sad that I was counting. My ears were now not listening to the many stories I had heard hundreds of times before. I noticed a battered Mini pull up outside, screeching to a stop. A small balding man got out and walked to our door. He must have been in his twenties. He knocked quietly on the glass, trying to get Lynn's attention.

Lynn opened the door and asked what he wanted.

"I have locked myself out of the house… can I borrow your key?" he asked.

She introduced Ben to me and gave him a key. He was polite and friendly. Not the person that Lynn had described so many times before. He spoke softly and seemed quite effeminate. A small weedy sort of person, truly loved and spoilt by his Mother.

I did wonder whether Ben's partner, Alex, was male or female. Ben took the keys and drove off, giving me a chance to slip away too.

In the late 1980s, many people were involved in property development, even my postman, often bragging to me how much he was making by converting old run-down houses into flats.

I decided that this might be a good idea, although, didn't have the funds to do so. I spoke to Terry about it, and he was also keen on the idea. Joining resources would stand us a better chance on getting a bank loan together, to try and start this project.

A successful meeting with our bank manager gave us the start we needed. A budget of fifty-thousand pounds.

We started hunting for a suitable property, without success. Having made a decision not to buy from our own Estate Agency, limited our market, however, we both thought that it would be more ethical to buy elsewhere. It was clear that competitive agents had their own established developer clients to sell the 'Project Properties' to.

Months went, with a bank loan in hand, burning a hole in our pockets, without even of a sniff of a suitable project to buy.

A retired couple came into our office with a set of keys to a large house they inherited in Cobham road. They were old clients of ours, Mr and Mrs Pymer. Having successfully moved this couple before, they were pleased with the service and were keen to instruct us to sell this old vacant house.

Mr Pymer, a retired, and very pedantic civil servant, had ill-fitting false teeth, that stayed closed as his mouth moved to talk. Mrs Pymer hardly spoke and had a 'fuck off' face. This was an expression my old Police Sergeant used to say, and stuck with me.

The large house in Cobham Road was completely derelict, with ivy growing all the way up to the gutters. The inside hadn't been touched for years, leaving it very dated, in need of a complete refurbishment. The windows were wedged shut and front door almost impossible to see. I noticed a few large cracks in the side, running up and down the walls.

Many viewings later on this run-down giant of a house, we introduced several developer buyers, all of which pulled out.

This was very disappointing, as I had spent many hours showing them around. It appeared the reason for each one pulling out, was that they were put off by the cracks in the walls, possible thinking it could be subsidence. Each developer didn't want to have the expense of a structural engineer's report.

The Pymers came in to see me to check on progress. I explained the situation and suggested that they either have an engineer's report done, to high light any potential problems, or place the property in an auction. Mr Pymer bit my head off at this suggestion, and even Mrs Pymer was cringing as if I had offered her a turd on a stick.

We continued our efforts for another month. Ironically, I was asked to value the house diagonally opposite the Pymers' house. The vendor was elderly and had a good grip of the knowledge of this road. I noticed a similar crack in his house and asked about it. The vendor told me that some houses in this road were 'bomb' damaged during the second world war, with many resulted in having cracks. He then showed me an engineer's report, clearly high lighting the bomb blast problems in this area. This was music to my ears as we can now be more confident to sell the Pymers' house.

The following day, The Pymers came into the office and I furnished them with this new fantastic, information, suggesting that they instruct an engineer to prove that the house was not subsiding. I even obtained a quote, eight hundred pounds. "Money well spent to finally get a sale on the house," I said.

This was flatly refused. The 'fuck off' face looked daggers at me, and Mr Pymer nearly spat his teeth out. They instructed me to carry on as we were.

After contacting previous applicants, providing them with this new information, none of them was interested.

I had a plan to perhaps buy the house with Terry as our first project. After much thought, we instructed the engineer ourselves and soon had a satisfactory report, confirming that the cracks were due to a bomb blast, thirty metres away, during the second world war. We invited the Pymers back to the office to discuss our plan. They came in straight away and were excited that we were even interested. Mrs Pymer cracked a rare smile. They accepted our offer of the full asking price and were delighted that we weren't going to charge any commission.

We shook hands, pleased that our first project was on the starting blocks. Completion took place two months later. During the process of buying the house, I obtained costs from local builders to refurbish the property. This was a daunting experience, as the costs were far more than I expected. It was soon clear that we now owned a house and couldn't afford to make it habitable, let alone make it a fantastic, fully refurbished home.

This showed our lack of experience and could end as a huge mistake. To make matters worse the property market was heading towards a recession. Panic was setting in with me as the bank loan charged had now kicked in. We have to sell the house and cut our losses.

The Pymers walk past our office every day, looking in between the window displays, like the cats that got the cream, with smirks on their faces. They must have thought that we were a real pair of mugs.

Terry and I decided to place the 'White Elephant' into the next local auction, along with the engineer's report, for any potential buyers to look at.

I spent a whole bank holiday weekend removing all the ivy from the house with a couple of mates. It looked so much better, giving me some confidence in being able to sell it in the forthcoming auction.

Auction day came, and we decided to attend to see what the dump of the house eventually sells for. We arrived at the hotel hosting the auction, and sat near the front. The attendance seemed poor, with only around thirty people there.

Properties were being sold in quick succession, some not even reaching the reserve price. There was a tap on my shoulder. I turned round to see the Pymers were sitting behind us.

"We thought we would just come along and see what the house sells for," Mr Pymer said smugly.

Terry and I couldn't believe it. We were pleasant to them, and waited patiently for our 'lot' to come up.

Terry nudged me and said, "We're next mate."

At the same time, the Pymers were tapping our shoulders saying, "Here we go."

Bidding started off slowly, starting at thirty-five thousand pounds, gradually creeping up to forty thousand. At this time my hands were sweating and heart beating like a drum. I was sure we were about to lose a lot of money. The Pymers were breathing down our necks, whispering to each other. The bidding crept up to fifty thousand pounds and paused for a while. I thought the hammer was going to come down, then suddenly the pace picked up, introducing telephone bids, with the bidding shooting up to seventy thousand.

I was having mixed feelings about this. In one hand I wanted to sell the house at a high price, and make a profit, and on the other hand, I didn't want the Pymers to think we had stitched them up.

The hammer went down at ninety-four thousand pounds. Terry and I were stunned, both wanting to jump into the air cheering, however, we had the Pymers behind us. I glanced behind for a second, they both looked pissed off. Terry and I kept quiet and continued watching the next lot being auctioned. A harder tap on my shoulder, the Pymers want my attention.

"Here we go," I thought.

I turned to see the Pymers, extending their hands out to shake ours. "Well done you two, excellent result," Mr Pymer said.

I replied, "Thank you. We weren't expecting that price. We just wanted to get our money back."

He responded, "You deserve it, both of you took the risk and it came up trumps for you. You did advise us to go to auction but we didn't listen."

The trip back to the office found us both cheering.

The Pymers became much friendlier after the auction, and instructed us to sell Mrs Pymer's late Mother's bungalow. They also recommended us to sell a house for a close friend of theirs.

My Dad's advice was to always be honest and leave a bit for someone else, came into my head.

With a profit and the bank paid back made us hungry for another project. During the Summer, I noticed an auction catalogue advertising a large derelict house in Ramuz Drive. We arranged viewing with the auctioneer, who met us at the property. A completely run-down house occupied by a recuse for many years who recently died there. As I walked in the smell was overwhelming. The condition was so bad the auctioneer wouldn't even come inside. I scurried around as quickly as possible, holding my breath. There were piles of rubbish and newspapers reaching the ceiling in most rooms. Hundreds of bags of human excrement were placed under floorboards within the rafters. Each room was like an obstacle course with some floorboards not put back down. The bathroom was unusable, with a broken bath full of old bottles and tins. The toilet was disgusting, the worst I have ever seen, or likely to see.

Terry shuffled out quickly, gagging, kicking the sea of debris out the way. I followed, glad to be out in the fresh air. The side gate was locked, but with gentle persuasion fell apart, giving access to the rear jungle. The growth of all the weeds, trees and bushes was immense, well over our heads. It was unknown how long the garden was at this stage.

Despite all the mess and smell, this property would be a great project as could be easily converted into two flats.

Terry wasn't too keen on this house, however, after obtaining builders quotes, could see that a profit could be made if we bought at the right price. I arranged to meet Claire, the architect, at the house, who turned up in her usual long dress and cardy. She had her trademark wicker basket, carrying her paperwork and tape measure. She tottered inside on her high heeled shoes, scanning the piles of rubbish.

"I am not going in any further until you get it cleared," she said. Really, I don't blame her.

Our builder was already inside, taking measurements, keen to do the job. The neighbours came out to find out what was going on. It must have looked strange watching two guys in suits, and an elderly lady with a wicker basket wandering around the site. The advice from our team of professionals was fairly positive.

After much discussion, we decided to bid for it in auction the following week. A maximum price was agreed and set in stone. It seemed a long wait before the auction date loomed upon us, but during this time the building costs for the conversion and renovations had been finely tuned. It was also pleasing that the auction company had arranged to have the house completely cleared and disinfected.

We arrived at the auction, based in the usual hotel. Sitting in the same seats as we sat at the last auction. We noticed that the room was getting very busy. Lots of people were coming in, before long all seats were taken. It was much nicer without the Pymers breathing down our necks. The lot we wanted was almost the last one, so we had a long wait ahead of us.

It turned out to the hottest day of the year, and after an hour or so, people were getting too hot and decided to leave. By the time our lot came up, there was only about a dozen people in attendance.

The lack of bidders in the room worked in our favour, as the hammer went down on our lot, at a price far lower than we thought. The Auctioneer said as the hammer went down. "Rather you than me. Good luck with this one, you'll need it!" With that comment wringing in my ears, it made me more determined to turn this around and develop two lovely flats, and ultimately make a profit.

Completion took place, kick-starting a hive of activity, with an Army of builders and landscapers completely gutting the place. Within weeks of hard graft, the whole house and garden were looking much better, although still had a long way to go.

Six months later, the project was finished, with two very saleable luxury flats, with all the correct planning permission, and new leases. Each flat looked superb, with fully tiled bathrooms, and beautifully fitted kitchens. The whole of the ground floor had new floorboards and replastered walls.

The new carpets finished off the project. Now we were ready for marketing, so smart colour brochures were prepared and distributed.

I showed over five people on the first day. Strangely I could faintly smell the sewage that was so bad when we first saw the house. Luckily nobody else noticed it. 'Perhaps it was in my head' I thought.

The ground floor sold straight away to Tim Bird. He was a young lad that worked in London, enjoying the process of buying his first property. Tim became a bit of a nightmare as he wanted some extras, and colour changes in some of the rooms. After changing some of the colours to his choice, he then wanted a patio built and polished floors in the sitting room. We could not agree to do this and suggested he arranged the extra work directly with the builder.

Tim had a small hissy fit in our office because he couldn't understand that all the extras that he demanded would have to be paid for by him, after exchange of contract. Terry politely said, "Please don't get into a 'flap' about it. When it's your flat you can do all the things you want in your own time."

This didn't go down well with him either. He spoke to us as if we had just come in on his shoe, which was unfair, because we had done everything that he requested. I saw red, getting annoyed with him and his attitude. I listened to him ranting for a while then said, "Unless you exchange now, the flat will go back onto the market."

His response was fairly hostile, however, he did go ahead and exchange contracts, and move in.

The first floor flat sold to twin spinsters, in their sixties. Miss Helen Clarke and Miss Hattie Clarke. They were a delight to deal with, having no complications. They had a small Pug called Popeye, which seemed appropriate as his eyes were sticking out of his head, looking in different directions. The twins were identical, even in their clothes and manner. The ladies would both speak at the same time, saying exactly the same thing, like stereo. They had a good sense of humour, although, sometimes bickering with each other over the slightest detail.

I leant over to pat Popeye on his head, and the twins said in unison. "Mind you don't pat him too hard as his eyes might pop out!"

He actually tried to bite me as my hand approached him.

The twins were like a pair of 'pepper pots', waddling in and out of the office, sometimes coming in just for a chat.

They moved into their flat a week after Tim Bird, keeping up their routine of popping into the office. It was nice to hear that the ladies got on well with Tim downstairs.

Several years later. Tim Bird had decided to sell his flat and buy a bigger property, so he invited me around to value his flat one evening.

As I walked into his sitting room, I could smell a faint sewage whiff. This reminded me of how bad this flat was when we first bought it. The flat was kept in lovely condition throughout, with a recently landscaped garden, shared with the twins upstairs. I placed the flat onto the market at a reasonable price to sell quickly. Tim had found a house to buy in Eastwood and told me that he was planning to marry his fiancé in eight months.

To my surprise a few days later the twins made an appointment to see me at the office. I was wondering what they wanted, as they walked in, and sat in front of my desk.

They both spoke together, with great excitement. I could hardly keep up with them. They soon calmed down, and I established that they were cash buyers, keen to buy Tim's flat at the full asking price.

"Popeye can't manage the stairs anymore, so we need to get on the ground floor as soon as possible," Helen or Hattie said. The transaction was agreed, leading to a quick completion, within eight weeks. Sadly, Popeye died a month after they moved downstairs. The twins told me that they lived in a flat each for a few weeks, but missed each other too much so they both ended up together downstairs, where they lived happily for the next fifteen years. Sadly, the twins died within a few weeks of each other, leaving the flat to their Nephew.

I was invited by their Nephew to value the flat for probate purposes, and when I met him there, I could still smell that same sewage whiff in the sitting room.

One Saturday morning, a valuation had been booked in. Terry asked me to accompany him to it, as he had just taken delivery of his new car, and wanted to show it off. We had a comfortable ride in his new car, pulling up at some traffic lights, showing red.

The lights turned green, and the car jerked forward and stalled to a halt. Terry turned the key to try and get it started without success. Terry tried again, flooding the car, still not starting. Getting annoyed and impatient, he tried again, still no joy. The chap behind started honking. A short pause and another failed attempted to start, with the honking behind becoming more consistent. Beep beep beep… Terry got out of the car and lent down to the window of the honking man, and shouted, "I'll tell you what. You sit in my car and try and get the fucking thing started, and I'll sit in your car and lean on the horn… you twat!"

The honking stopped, and thankfully the car started, and we were on our way.

We arrived at the appointment address, and measured up and took photos. The vendor was busy making cakes for her son's birthday party, set for the afternoon. We attracted attention from the vendor's eight-year-old son, who followed us around asking questions, and showing us his balloons with figure eight on it, and a spiderman one too.

Almost finishing the instruction, just as I was photographing the kitchen, extending from the dining area, I saw Terry pop a freshly baked child-size Rice Krispy cake into his mouth, whilst the vendor was taking another tray of cakes out of the oven.

She suddenly turned to put the tray onto the worktop, and said to Terry, "What do you think of my house then?"

Terry looked very uncomfortable, like a small child that had been caught with his hand in the biscuit tin. His cheeks were puffed out with Rice Krispie cake, going red and desperately trying to reply. "Well… err …" he muffled, turning to me, hoping I would cut in.

I interjected, "It's a lovely house with some nice features. It will suit many families."

The vendor turned to me to carry on the conversation, whilst Terry hurriedly swallowed the offending cake.

The appointment successfully came to a close, with us both wishing the little lad a happy birthday, and the vendor having no idea of the missing cake. Just as I was putting the camera back into its case, the little boy said to his Mum. "That man ate one of my cakes!!"

"Don't be silly Robby, he wouldn't do that," she replied, as we were edging towards the door.

We couldn't get out of the house quick enough, with the boy still insisting there was a missing cake.

"He has such an imagination," she said, trying to shut her son up.

"That was close," Terry said, as we got in the car, handing me a chocolate Rice Krispy cake he had pocketed. "Thought you might like one too?"

The following Monday the vendor came into the office with her signed copy of our terms and conditions. The little boy was holding a small paper bag with string handles and handed it to Terry.

The lady said. "I have brought you some of Robby's birthday cake, hope you like it?"

We both said. "Thank you, Robby. Hope you enjoyed your party?"

An appointment in the office with Michael Blake in the afternoon was quite an eye-opener for me. Mary made the appointment and mentioned at the time that he seemed a bit strange. I wasn't sure what to expect.

The door opened, and in walked a ma about my age asking for me. I got up, introducing myself and shook hands with him, noticing that his eyes were looking in different directions. He sat at my desk and I politely asked. "What can I do for you?"

He replied. "My name is Mmm… Mmm… Michael Ber… Ber… Blake, and I am looking for a Ber… Ber…" I interjected, "A bungalow?"

"Nnn… N… no, a buy to let," he replied.

"Ok, what price are you looking up to?" I asked, as he produced a letter from his pocket. The letter was from his Solicitor, confirming that Mr Blake had won over one million pounds in an industrial injury compensation claim. I read through the letter and realised that he had been medically discharged from work.

I produced some leaflets of suitable properties that would be ideal for letting purposes.

Michael flipped through various brochures, selecting some that he thought would be suitable. I agreed, offering to take him to see them. He didn't want to view any, finding it difficult to express himself as he wasn't able to find the words.

He partly gave up, miming at me still looking at opposite walls. The sight was quite strange, however, I tried my best to understand him, without making him feel awkward or embarrassed.

He put three brochures side by side on my desk, like playing cards. All similar properties at the same price. Funnily he chose the exact houses that I would have chosen.

"So which one would you like to buy?" I asked.

"All of them, p… p… please," he said.

"You want to buy all three?" I asked, trying to clarify.

"Yes, all th… th… three," he replied, putting three fingers up to my face.

"Ok, I will just fill in a few forms, then contact your Solicitor to get things started," I replied, rather surprised.

Although Michael had been through the mill with health issues, he knew what he wanted, and was easy to deal with.

As he got up to go, he noticed a picture of a bungalow in our window display.

"I want that too…" he said, pointing at a picture of a bungalow. He then walked out of the office to cross the road. I went after him, asking if he really wanted the bungalow as well?

Firstly, he didn't ask the address, secondly, he didn't ask the price.

"Are you sure you are happy to proceed on the bungalow as well?" I asked.

"Yes," he replied, walking away.

I was a bit stunned. Theoretically, I have just sold four properties, subject to contract, in half an hour, with very little effort.

For some reason, I didn't believe for one minute that these transactions would go through. I was wrong, within two months, Michael came into the office to collect his keys to all four properties, and was delighted with his choices. My colleagues were shocked at the speed and reliability of the purchases.

My Dad used to say, "Never judge a book by its cover."

Eight

We were instructed to market 'Jokers Wild', the house Stuart pointed out to me during my first weeks as an Estate Agent.

This was a substantial property in one of the most prestigious locations in this part of Essex. This house was every Estate Agent's dream instruction. The Vendor, however, was every Estate Agent's nightmare. Tom Black, a local, well-known property developer. He was a tall East London, self-made millionaire that possibly walked over many people to get where he is now. His appearance was similar to a 'Bond Villain'. He insisted on having things done his way, and his way only. Other agents probably didn't want to deal with him, however, I thought this might be a good challenge for me.

Tom Black only wanted Terry or me to conduct viewings on his property while he was there to oversee it. We followed instructions to the tee, meeting pre-arranged clients at 'Jokers Wild'. This was not the best way to sell this house, as Tom Black would take over the viewing leaving either Terry or me to stand around like a lemon. Tom Black was not the easiest person to get on with. The banter between him and the prospective buyer would sometimes end up with Tom Black being very blunt, or even rude.

He would say. “Can you afford this house? or, “Is this a day out?”

Often offending people would result in failing to find a buyer.

Normal questions would be asked, “What are your neighbours like?”

The reply would be. “I don’t have anything to do with them, although a Doctor lives next door.”

I found that if Tom Black struck up a bond with someone, he would be fine, and reasonably polite, however, if their face didn’t fit he would be rude and arrogant.

An Indian couple, Mr and Mrs Hussain came to view one Saturday morning. I got there five minutes early to assess the vendor’s mood. The Hussains were driving from Surrey and were running late, which wasn’t a good start.

Mr Black was already in a foul mood, so the lateness didn’t help. A dark blue Bentley pulled up onto the sweeping gravel drive that wrapped around a flamboyant three-tier fountain, gushing at least twenty feet of water into the air. This was only activated when prospective buyers were coming to view.

I greeted the Hussains and their two children and introduced them to Mr Black. They were extremely polite, apologising for their late arrival. Mr Black ushered them around his house, showing very little interest in them. Mr Hussain asked valid questions directly to Mr Black, who replied in a ‘brushing off’ fashion. I tried to continue with the answers to try and satisfy Mr Hussain. I was getting the impression that Mr Black was a bit racist, and I certainly didn’t want the Hussains to pick up on that.

Forty minutes or so later, the viewing was over and Mr Hussain asked Mr Black if any of the furniture was included in the price. Mr Black leaned his towering structure into Mr Hussain's personal space and said forcefully whilst pointing his finger right in his chest, "Now look here Gandhi, I am selling the house. Not my home!!" I was taken aback but not at all surprised, knowing how Mr Black can lose his temper quite quickly.

It was well known that he struck a traffic warden and charged with assault a year ago. The local newspapers were full of it, in great detail.

Mr Hussain looked shocked at his behaviour and retreated with his family to his Bentley. I followed apologising for my vendor's outburst. I felt genuinely embarrassed for the Hussains as they were a nice family. They told me that they were cash buyers and would have bought the house, but couldn't have had dealings with Mr Black. Quite frankly, I did not blame them. Most of the viewings on this house went the same way. I offered to do the viewings without the vendors being there, as I thought that people were being put off by him. 'Jokers Wild' remains on the market.

A few weeks later, another viewing was booked in. It was arranged that I meet Captain Roger Yardley Hall at 'Jokers Wild'.

As usual, I arrived a few minutes early to assess the mood of Mr Black. The fountain was activated, spurting water to a great height, the dog put into an outside kennel, and coffee percolating on the Aga. Mrs Black was very accommodating, offering me a cup of coffee and a biscuit. A Range Rover swept onto the drive and pulled up next to my car. A dapper gentleman stepped out, smartly dressed in a dark blue suit, crisp white shirt and trainers. A strange combination of dress, I thought. Who wears trainers with a suit? Each to their own.

The banter between The Captain and Mr Black started well. They seemed to get on straight away, with normal questions being sensibly answered.

The Captain walked all over the house and grounds, seemingly to be quite taken with what he saw, and happy with the layout, style and décor.

He walked to the bottom of the garden with Mr Black holding back to speak to me.

"Do you think he can afford my house? I won't drop from one million one hundred and fifty thousand pounds you know!"

"He told the office he was looking up to one and a half million pounds, so let's see whether he likes it and makes an offer," I replied.

I remembered my Dad's theory of people that kept their military title in civilian life, are normally a bit dodgy and full of their own self-importance.

The viewing ended in the front garden, walking around the lawned areas surrounded by a mass of shrubs and flowering plants. Whilst the Captain and Mr Black were in deep conversation my attention was drawn to the Range Rover. I noticed a sticker in the back window, clearly stating in small print, 'Prestige Auto Hire. 'with various numbers and website. I wrote this information onto my file. I also noticed a Pilots uniform hanging from the hand pull over the rear seat, also a matching hat next to it. I had a strange feeling about the client.

Mr Black noticed the uniform hanging in the back of the car and said, "So you are a pilot then?"

"Yes. I am a commercial airline pilot, mainly based at Stanstead Airport," he replied.

This status seemed to impress Mr Black, who was on his best behaviour, perhaps thinking that he had a buyer for his house. The Captain seemed to be lapping up the attention he was receiving from the Blacks.

They carried on chatting away for ages. I was standing around, ignored by both parties.

This gave me an opportunity to look closely at the pilot's suit. It looked like a poor-quality fancy dress hire outfit, as if hired for a function.

A full asking price offer had been arranged between the two parties. Hands were shaking and excitement was in the air.

The Captain walked across the gravel drive in his scruffy trainers to his car. "I will be in touch," he stated.

"I hope not," I said under my breath.

Mr Black was smirking with delight, obviously thinking he had pulled off a great deal with his Captain friend.

The next day I rang the Captain on his only number, a mobile. He confirmed that he wanted to buy 'Jokers Wild' and offered me his Solicitors details. I asked him to supply me with the usual forms of ID, and also proof that he was a cash buyer, as he said he was.

Before he would give me this information, he asked if he could go back to the house on Saturday for another look.

The Captain pulled up into the same parking space in an Aston Martin DB9. He got out wearing the same suit and well-worn trainers.

I couldn't help myself, so I edged towards the rear of the car and noticed the same 'Prestige Auto Hire' sticker in the back window.

Another hour of Mr Black and the Captain walking all over the property, supping coffee, talking bullshit to each other was beginning to annoy me, as deep down I knew I was wasting my time. Although the Blacks were delighted with the progress and impressed with the dashing airline pilot that wanted to buy their wonderful house.

I should have been excited by this. The best house on the market, a full price offer and a huge commission when it completes. My colleagues at the office were more excited than me. I just couldn't put my finger on the problem. I didn't seem to ring true. Do I let the Blacks know of my feelings, after all, they are my clients, and paying our bill. I had a duty to let Mr Black know my feelings, so I rang him and explained my concerns. I was immediately slapped down by him, saying that I hadn't gained the experience that he has, as he for some reason trusted the Captain.

My concerns were highlighted over the next few weeks, as the information I asked for many times never appeared. Promises of the I. D being with me the next day never happened. I checked out the 'Prestige Auto Hire' website and both cars that the Captain drove were featured as bold as brass with full-colour photos.

The home address the Captain gave me was 'Drayton Manor', situated on the Norfolk, Suffolk borders. I wanted to investigate this further, so I decided that on my next day off I will go and see for myself.

I mentioned this to the rest of the staff, who didn't share the same feelings as me. They thought I was just being paranoid.

Another week went by with still no ID. Also, the Captain's Solicitor had a similar response to me.

My day off led me to drive to Suffolk to see for myself.

I found 'Drayton Manor' quite easily. It wasn't a Manor at all. It was an unimpressive detached Victorian house with a large bed and breakfast sign outside.

Totally what I didn't expect. This raised my suspicions even more, to a whole new level.

I was thinking on my journey back on the A12. "So what have I got here?"

A so-called Captain.

Flashy hired cars.

Smart suit with scruffy trainers.

A pilot's outfit, possibly fake.

A month gone by without ID.

No Solicitors instructed.

Does this a man have illusions of grandeur?

Is this a con man?

Is he a nutter?

Did he own the bed and breakfast?

Why did he not answer my phone calls? Is it because he is a pilot and couldn't take my call?

I managed to contact him one evening, out of office hours using my wife mobile, so he wouldn't recognise my number. I could tell he was a bit surprised and even annoyed that it was me on the phone.

He went into full bullshit mode. He was good at it, leaving me unsure whether he was genuine or not.

Mr Black was also getting impatient, so I told him again of my suspicions. This was received with disappointment understandably. The property was placed back onto the market.

My curiosity got the better of me. I didn't want to let this go. I wanted to know what this Captain was all about, and what his intentions were.

I told a friend who happens to be a Police Inspector, telling him of my dilemma with this 'so-called Captain'. Thoughts were running through my head. Have I got this wrong? Am I going to make a prat of myself?

I was also upset that the sale of 'Jokers Wild' had slipped through my fingers.

A few days later my Police friend rang me with an update at around ten pm.

My mind was put at rest when I heard those words.

"The Captain isn't a Captain at all. He has been wanted for a while, although I can't tell you too much at this stage, but, what I will say is that he is a con man, embezzling wealthy retired people, by posing as a financial advisor, offering gilt-edge investments. His real name is Roger Hall. He is also wanted in France as well as the UK."

It all came to light a few months later when the con man would impress wealthy people, presenting them with impressive glossy brochures, taking them out for expensive meals in hired flashy cars, and generally given a successful appearance.

It seemed many people were suckered in, investing large sums of money with him. This money would go straight into his bank and every month he would send a dividend to the unsuspecting victim, showing that the 'investment' is too good to be true. Most victims were happy with this not realising the extent of the con. Some victims were so pleased they would 'invest' further large sums of money.

Mr Hall's luck ran out when an investor died, leaving the Solicitor acting for the probate with difficulties collecting the money from the investment fund. Alarm bells rang, resulting in a Police investigation. Mr Hall went on the run for several years, continuing to con people with various other scams. I followed with interest the forthcoming court case, finding Mr Hall guilty, resulting in a long sentence at Her Majesty's pleasure.

I could only assume that the air pilot's uniform was a prop for another scam.

I should have been a bit miffed by losing a potential sale on this landmark property, however, I was pleased that my suspicions were correct and ultimately prevented further people being conned by this man.

After this experience, my outlook on people changed, almost judging them on initial appearance, which I know is wrong.

Over the next few months, the Blacks were a bit sore from being taken in by this con man, but at least they didn't lose any money. They took 'Jokers Wild' off the market and decided to stay and build an orangery onto the rear of the house.

Nine

I managed to get an offer accepted on one of Richard's flats, to a first-time buyer called Nigel Middleton.

He was a nervous and very pedantic person, watching at every step of the way with the progress of the build.

The building itself was almost finished, with Nigel's choice of kitchen units and appliances all freshly installed. The only choice left for Nigel was the bathroom suite. Nigel made an appointment to see me in the office to look at the brochures and discuss the choice of colours.

We agreed a time and as usual, he arrived in his normal punctual fashion, clutching his 'property file' in his normal organised fashion. He is the only person I know that has his own customised hard hat with his name on it.

Richard had phoned me earlier that morning, stressing that his building team had already installed a cream coloured bathroom suite. I knew this could be a big problem with Nigel, as one of the reasons he chose this flat is that he would be able to choose his kitchen and bathroom. The kitchen installation was bad enough, with Nigel drawing out in great detail, layout, colours and white goods. Eventually, it was installed within allowance to Nigel's satisfaction.

Nigel sat down, opening his folder, each room colour coded. He flipped to the bathroom page and said.

"I know the developers want my final choice for the bathroom suite colours."

"Ok, I have some choices for you Nigel. There is cream, off-white, bamboo, champagne, pampas and oatmeal," I said, hoping he will like one of these.

He pondered for a while, flipping through his colour chart, and eventually made a decision. "This is all my choice, is it?" he asked.

I replied. "Yes, you have six choices… which one do you like?" I was beginning to panic, thinking he may have rumbled my plan.

"Cream… Yes, definitely cream," he said with great excitement in his voice.

I replied. "Ok, I will arrange that for you. Cream with contrasting tiles."

While these negotiations were being discussed, I could see Terry with his head in his hands, possibly feeling my stress. Lulu piped up when Nigel left the office.

"Well, that was easy, well done."

Nigel moved in a month later, delighted with his choices. He also became the secretary of the management committee, when all the neighbouring flats became occupied.

Later that evening we had already arranged to go out for a meal, with our partners to celebrate a successful quarter.

We all met at a local Italian Restaurant, 'Dolce Vita', at seven o'clock. None of us had been there before, so, we were all looking forward to this experience.

The date had been in our diaries for a few weeks, with the girls in the office talking of nothing else. Dress styles and hairdos were the main topics of the conversation. The guys all decided to wear suits, as the venue was known for being 'upmarket' and adopted a smart dress code.

We all entered into a small reception area, greeted by two tall, dark-haired Italian waiters, neatly dressed in black evening suits with bowties to match.

I noticed straight away that these two waiters completely ignored all the men, focusing their full attention on the ladies. Their coats were taken and hung up. Chairs were pulled out for them and drinks were offered. The Italian accent seemed falsely strong, as they both spoke very quickly in a projected voice, changing tone to a much quieter voice.

"Whata woulda you lika to drink? We have da lovely red a vino for you beautiful ladies," one waiter asked with his hand on Carly's arm. The other waiter was oozing charm onto Mary. "Could I getta you a nica Gina and Tonico beautiful lady?" The ladies were lapping up the attention.

At least ten minutes of slushy charm and innuendos poured over the ladies in our party.

I thought I heard one of the waiters say in a low, fast, deep, Italian speaking voice. "Howa about the lady wid da biggy boobies, whata would you lika?"

At first, I thought that I had misheard the waiter, having such a strong accent, and with the noise of the restaurant. Lulu was sitting at the head of the table as he is such a big guy, he took up a large space. His shirt seemed too small for his huge bulking torso. I heard the tallest waiter ask Lulu, in the usual off-hand manner. "Whata woulda you wanna drink, a beer or a de coka cola or justa tap water?"

"A Peroni please," he answered politely, unaware of the waiter's off-hand style.

I butted in saying, "All the guys will have Peroni, please."

The waiter looked at me as if I were an alien from another planet.

"I coma to you in a minito," he snapped.

Under his breath he said, "I ama dealing wid dis ugly cretin."

I am sure I was the only person to hear his rudeness and realised that these two clowns were taking the piss out of us, and having a good laugh at our expense.

The drinks order was finally completed. The party were enjoying the chat and drinks. The girls were saying how lovely the waiters were. Little did they know that we were all targets of the humour.

We were all given a comprehensive menu, written in Italian. Prompted by a smirking waiter who asked us if we would like him to translate.

"We hava da porchetta wid a da pasta, nduja wid ricotta, spaghetti wid porcini mushrooms or pizza wid a many toppings." This was quite overwhelming, as most of us were enjoying a new experience. The choice of so many dishes delighted the party, loving the attention from these 'hands-on' waiters. The ladies ordered first, I caught the eye of one of the waiters looking at his colleague with a smile. They were both having a good laugh at us. My attention should have been focused on my party, however, I was listening and watching the behaviour of our waiters.

Most meal orders were taken without too much confusion. Then it came to Lulu's turn, who was obviously unsure what to have. The waiter appeared to help by offering suggestions.

"We canna do you a lasagne wid a da garlic bread." Then in a low almost whispering voice, "Or a de fishy fingers wid chippies." Luckily Lulu didn't hear the last choice. The second waiter was trying not to laugh.

Eventually, everyone was presented with the correct meal. Some dressing was deliberately spilt over Lulu, still unaware of the sloppy service we were getting from these two clowns.

Side orders were twisted to sound like a rude word, providing much amusement to the waiters.

We were all eating and enjoying the meal. I excused myself for a bathroom break. I had to walk past the bar area to find the gents just off the reception hall.

As I walked past the bar, clearly hearing these two clowns talking in normal English accents, with a slight Birmingham twang to it. They didn't see me as they were bending down restocking the bar. These guys weren't Italian at all.

"We need to order some more lagers, Dave," waiter one said to waiter two.

Waiter two replied, "Yes mate, and also we are out of lemons."

I stood there for a while listening to their banter. Suddenly waiter one turned around and saw me there. "Can a I helpa you?" he said, unsure how long I had been there.

"Yes, you can, Dave. I would like Brandies, all round, and to be able to walk out of here with my party without a bill. I'm sure you understand!" I said, rather annoyed.

Dave went bright red, and so did his piss-taking pal. They looked deflated at each other and looked at me shrugging their shoulders.

I then said. "I can get the fish finger-eating, ugly cretin, at the end of the table if you like. Or the lady with the big boobies. Perhaps you would like to explain to them?"

The cocky smirks fell from their faces, as they both realised that they had been rumbled.

"So Brandies all round then?" Dave said, picking up a bottle from the bar.

The style of service changed dramatically for the rest of the evening. No more silly innuendos, or rude puns. We were served with coffee, without the waiters dancing attendance over the ladies. We all got up to leave without a bill appearing, with my colleagues asking about how we split the bill. I was pleased to say that it was already taken care of. I told them about the waiters when we were back at work.

The next March I took my Dad and Stepmum there for Dad's sixty-third birthday. The waiters recognised me and spoke perfect English all evening, attending to us in a perfectly reasonable way.

Dad said to Dave, "Last time I came here, about six months ago, you guys could hardly speak English, so you have done really well to become fluent in such a short space of time. Well done!"

I winked at Dave, who gave us a complimentary bottle of wine and a heavily discounted bill.

During the meal, Dad mentioned that he has a Parrott in the surgery with one leg. His aim was to make a false leg, as the Parrott was getting older, and having trouble balancing on his only leg. The owner of this Parrott was a local well-known Antique dealer, who's life revolved around his trusted feathered friend.

Dad had tried several times to build a leg out of medical splints, without success. I offered to help and perhaps carve one from a piece of strong wood.

This was welcomed as a last chance to be able to fix this problem. After a trip to the surgery to meet the patient, called 'Calypso', I took measurements and photos to try and get some idea of size and design.

Calypso was happily chatting away to himself and promptly told me to bugger off.

"Excuse his foul language," Dad said, whilst stroking his patient.

He was a fantastic looking Parrott, leaning awkwardly against the bars of a huge gold-coloured cage, gripping his perch with his remaining leg.

"Hello. What's your name then?" I asked.

Calypso looked at me with his head cocked to one side. "Bollocks... What's yours... Ha ha?" He replied.

After much discussion, Dad and I found a possible way to save this wonderful bird. I was to carve a leg from a dowel, and insert four metal claw-like rods for him to stand on a perch. I enjoyed woodworking, so over the weekend, I made a leg to the exact size. Lots of whittling and sanding and finally painting it in lead-free paints, it was beginning to actually look like a Parrott's leg.

I dropped the leg off to Dad, who, that day put Calypso under anaesthetic to be able to attach it to the remaining stump.

The process was very successful, with Calypso coming too, standing on his perch with perfect balance. I popped in to see him, with some excitement.

Calypso stood proudly on his perch, swaying from leg to leg happily squawking and shouting out the odd swear word, or telephone noise. We both stood out of sight and watched him, really to see if he was going to accept this new limb. It seemed to be highly suitable.

I went to see him, met with the usual torrent of abuse and foul language. "Hello, old chap... How are you?"

"Hello... Ugly sod," he replied.

"You are standing nice and straight now, Calypso," I said.

"Bugger off..." he squawked, turning his back with perfect balance.

I turned to leave wishing him luck with his new leg and shouted 'goodbye for now' to him.

He shouted back, "Thank you for my leg… now bugger off!"

The leg attracted much attention with the local press, stoked by the owner of Calypso, who was amazed by the outcome.

Several years later, I went into the Antique shop, scouting for a present for my Uncle, who collects snuff boxes. I saw Calypso in his cage, in pride of place in the shop. He had become quite a celebrity, enjoying every bit of the attention.

As I was looking around at the curios, Calypso must have recognised me and shouted. "Hello… Thank you for my leg… bugger off."

The owner was astonished, and he said that he has never said that before. He only normally swears, or, is rude to people.

A few years later, Dad retired and sadly went blind with Macular degeneration in both eyes. He never complained about his handicap, he carried on with normal life, waving his white stick about whilst crossing roads. Eventually, he was united with a wonderful Labrador guide dog called 'Kato'. His new lease of life started with more independence and a purpose in life, with dog walks and the responsibility of looking after his new friend.

As a treat, and to bring some sunshine into Dad's life, I took him to regular comedy evenings at the theatre, including pantomimes with his Grandchildren. Although he couldn't see, he could still enjoy the atmosphere. I managed to reserve front row seats, as the local theatre gave a concession to blind people.

One year, we went to see Cinderella pantomime with all the family, including excited children, pleased to be sitting two foot from the stage.

Buttons, played by Bobby Davro fired a glitter cannon into the audience as part of the performance, unfortunately for me, the cannon dropped most of the glitter on my head. I was covered in shiny, sparkly glitter to the great amusement of the children and the audience. This was not funny, especially having to sit through the rest of the show looking like a Christmas tree.

Finally, the panto finished, resulting in us all waiting by the stage door, as the children were keen to get some autographs. I left a trail of glitter behind me, I could even taste it. After a short wait, standing patiently with the children, while people were walking past me, laughing and pointing, Buttons appeared, apologising for the glitter stunt that went wrong. For many months after, I found glitter in my hair, with the further embarrassment of clients looking at my head and mentioning the glitter.

A month after the panto, I took my Dad and Stepmum to see Jim Davidson, a stand-up comedian, at the Cliffs Pavilion. Dad really enjoyed comedians and was looking forward to the evening, I suppose it was a release for him, as with stand-up comedy acts he could just sit there and take it all in, without having the upset of missing out watching a performance.

I knew that Jim Davidson was a lively comedian and thought that Dad and my Stepmum would like the show. Because I booked late we couldn't reserve the front seats, however, we managed to get into row 'J'.

I had seen Jim Davidson on TV, realising that those shows would have been edited to suit certain audiences, perhaps for different ages.

We arrived at our seats within a packed auditorium. Within the first minute, I was cringing at the language used by the comic, although I didn't mind, I was worried that Dad and my Stepmum may not be appreciating it. They were very old school and of that age being quite prudish, however, I think that Dad would secretly have liked a bit of alternative humour.

The next fifteen minutes were very blue. I snatched a sideways glance to see that my Stepmum was stony-faced, uncomfortable with the content of the show. I nudged Dad and whispered. "I don't think this is going down well. Do you think we should stay, or, shall we sneak out?"

He replied. "I think we should go."

We waited for a pause in the performance and got up, shuffling along the row of seated people, trying not to cause any attention. I steered Dad around peoples' feet as best as I could and shuffled him into the direction of the exit.

Suddenly the spotlight shone straight at us making our hasty exit. We were lit up like a beacon, with the whole audience watching our every move. Dad apologising to the people he was treading on, whilst trying to exit row 'J'. I hadn't noticed that Jim Davidson had gone completely silent whilst he was watching us trying to sneak out.

To my horror, the show was focused on us.

"Leaving already?" Came booming over the sound system.

Trying to ignore him, I heard the hum of laughter, then another blast from the comic.

"Too rude for your prudish taste then…? Go on Fuck off… go on off you go…"

We inched our way to the faintly marked exit sign in the full glare of the spotlight. I didn't know where to look. I had hold of Dad's arm whilst I guided him up a row of three steps, with his other arm free to stick his two fingers up at Jim Davidson. The audience was in hysterics with Dad's antics. I think Dad got the biggest laugh of the night, as he keeps reminding me at any opportunity.

I got back to the office to find a familiar face wandering around outside, looking at the vast array of properties in our window display. He was accompanied by a large young lady bearing a resemblance to 'Olive', from 'on the buses'.

We were all working peacefully at our desks, wondering if this old client would come in. They eventually entered the office, walking straight up to my desk.

"Remember me? I am deaf," said Gordon Parker. Whilst holding his girlfriend's hand, and pulling up seats.

"Oh yes. You bought a flat in Southsea Avenue a few years ago," I replied.

"I bought a flat in Southsea Avenue a few years ago," he said, repeating my statement.

The couple had caught the attention of the rest of the staff, who were all watching how this meeting was going to pan out.

"So, are you thinking of moving?" I asked.

"This is my fiancé, Ruth. She is also deaf. We are thinking of moving to somewhere a bit bigger," he said. They both politely extended their hands to shake mine, as, I was only too pleased to help them.

I heard Terry say under his breath. "I thought you were deaf, not blind!"

This comment was heard by everybody, luckily not by Gordon Parker and his fiancé. I could see out of the corner of my eye, Terry and Carly shuffling out of sight, trying to hold it together.

Gordon then proudly stated. "Ruth is expecting a baby, you see, so we really want a garden when we move."

I congratulated them both, offering my assistance when they decide to view some properties.

They left, excitedly with many leaflets to browse through.

The couple did eventually move to their dream home, just in time to welcome their baby boy. The couple were so pleased with the move, that they invited me to their wedding the following Spring.

Ten

A chance meeting with an old friend that shared ski holidays with me twenty years ago, brought a new aspect to my life.

My friend, Sid, now in his sixties, fit as a flea, and a qualified ski instructor. He asked me if I was interested in joining a group of instructors in joining him on a trip to Austria, to teach five disadvantaged young adults to ski.

I passed my ski instructors exam when I was in my early twenties, after many years of ski holidays instead of Summer holidays.

During my younger years, I would much rather ski than sit on a beach or by a pool.

After a few days, it was agreed that I would be the fifth member of the team. This would involve flying to Munich, and travel to Niederau, and become an instructor for ten days.

The organiser was an ex-Marine called Reg Meadon, who sadly lost both his legs in active service in Afghanistan. Now rather awkwardly, he walks on older style metal legs, without knee joints. He was one of the nicest guys I have ever met.

He was already in Austria, brushing up on his skibobbing. A skibob is basically a bicycle with skis instead of wheels. Reg was unable to balance on skis, so this was the next best way of being able to join in.

The day came round when I met the other three instructors at Stanstead Airport. Sid was first to greet me, introducing me to Dr Annie Hogan, a surgeon at Addenbrookes Hospital, a fantastic skier, once selected for the British ski team in her youth. Then Eddy Wall, known as 'Brick', a serving soldier in the British Army, and part of a motorcycle stunt team. Eddy was about my age, with a handicapped daughter who sadly died before she reached adulthood.

After a comfortable flight, we arrived at Munich Airport, collected our kit, and waited for Reg in the pick-up area.

We all heard a distant clanking sound. Reg appeared in the distance. Clank, clank, clank, as he approached us. It was Reg beaming from ear to ear, staggering over to our small group, extending his 'meat plate'-sized hand to greet us.

Reg introduced himself and led us to a minibus to continue our journey. We all piled in and started making a plan for the next ten days activities. Reg had organised this trip, so took charge. Since he left the Marines, he spent all his time fundraising for several charities. Even the cost of this trip was met by a charity set up by Reg. Normally these five disadvantaged adults would be lucky if they had a trip to the seaside for one day. Each young adult would have a carer to look after them when they weren't with us.

We all got on well from the start and formulated a plan to be able to provide the best possible time for these guys that were in our care during the next ten days.

Sid suggested that we start at 8a.m. and finish back at the bottom of the mountain at noon, where the carers would be waiting. We would then have the rest of the day to do what we wanted. This was all agreed during our swaying minibus ride, snaking through the snowy mountain roads.

We arrived at our hotel, known as 'Gusthof', at around 4p.m. We were greeted by Cheryl, the main carer for her party of excited lads, she politely called the 'Motley Crew'. They had arrived earlier that day and were still unpacking. We agreed to meet her and the other carers with the 'Motley Crew', in an hour, once we have all checked in.

The 'Gusthof' was a traditional four-storey chalet-style hotel, with a large reception area leading to a split-level sitting area, with leather chesterfields and low coffee tables. A very inviting room, with roaring log fire and views across to the mountain we were going to be skiing on the next day.

We arrived by a lift to the reception area to be met by Cheryl and her four carer friends. The five guys were standing in a line, pretty much in size order, similar to the children in the Sound of Music. The carers were quite clear that they didn't want to participate in the ski activities, they were keen to explore the coffee bars and gift shops whilst we were skiing.

The five guys, all with Downs syndrome, consisted of, Noisy Alan, Quiet Alan, Jerry, Freddie and Dave, all aged between twenty-four and thirty-one. We walked out of the lift together and introduced ourselves, with Reg attracting much attention with his strange walk.

None of these guys had been abroad before, so were overexcited with this new adventure. The Motley Crew giggled at Reg's strange walk as he staggered towards them, clanking and grinding.

Sid suggested we all have an evening meal together that evening, as we could get to know each other and decide who to pair up with for the ski activities. Noisy Alan ran around squeaking loudly with excitement, and Quiet Alan calmed him down, taking the sensible role. "Quieten down, Alan… people might think there is something wrong with you!!"

Cheryl and her four friends retired to the bar, knocking back the gluhwein, while we were getting to know the lads. We knew this was going to be an interesting time.

Eddy noticed a poster in the reception advertising a disco night in the town mid-week. "Hey guys, this looks fun. Shall we go and boogie?"

The Motley Crew seemed more excited about this than skiing. All five suddenly got up and started dancing about, knocking into other guests and tables, spilling drinks and making a scene. Norma, a large, bubbly carer came over and clapped her hands twice, controlling the lads back to their chairs. We called her 'Mary Poppins' after that.

The meal went well, giving us, as instructors an idea to the different personalities, strengths and needs of our pupils. The two Alans seemed inseparable, Jerry was nervous and very polite, Dave was in a dream world of his own and Freddie was full of energy, unable to keep still and talking non-stop.

The Hotel owner introduced himself to us.

"I am Clause. Am very pleased to meet you all. I hope you enjoy your stay here."

He was a tall Austrian with a large white handlebar moustache and small gold-rimmed glasses.

He continued to proudly tell us of other facilities we can use, to include a swimming pool and sauna in the basement. The tray of welcoming drinks he was holding was carefully placed onto our table.

"This is Schnapps. A well-known drink in Austria. Please accept this from me," he said.

The Schnapps came with tiny glasses. We all had a glass, not expecting it to taste like methylated spirits. The Motley Crew knocked it back without batting an eyelid.

The next day, after a breakfast of porridge and coffee, Annie rounded up the guys, pairing them to an instructor, that she thought would be beneficial to both people.

Jerry was paired with me, Annie with Dave, Freddie with Eddy, Noisy Alan with Sid, and Quiet Alan with Reg. The carers, slightly hungover from their intake of gluhwein, waved goodbye as we walked into the town to collect our skis and boots from the hire shop.

We were first in the ski hire shop. Boots were fitted, Skis supplied with sticks, and ski passes were clipped to our jackets. We all picked up our skis and sticks and negotiated our way through the narrow access way through the shop. Unfortunately, Jerry accidentally knocked a full rack of skis, resulting in an avalanche of skis falling like 'pick up sticks' onto the floor. Eddy and I scrambled to pick them up whilst the ski shop manager looked on with a miserable face.

The queue at the chair lift was already growing, so we joined it and clipped our skis onto our boots ready to board. The queue shuffled forward in an organised fashion, with Annie and Dave boarding first, then the others with Jerry and I bringing up the rear. I didn't make a big deal over this, as I knew that Jerry was very nervous. He held my arm as we edged towards the chairlift.

I gave Jerry instructions. "All you have to do is line up to the chair as it comes towards you and sit down and hold on."

We shuffled into place with the chair whipping us up into the air. Jerry screamed a bit. I pulled the safety bar down and we were away.

"Well done Jerry… See no problem," I said, looking at Jerry smiling, being very pleased with himself. He even asked if we can do it again.

"Yes. Of course, it is the only way up the mountain. We will ski down and do it all over again," I said with the cold air catching my breath. We could hear noisy Alan's booming voice a few chairs ahead of us. The views were outstanding. Pine treetops were swaying in the wind, dropping snow onto the skiers below.

"The trip is about ten minutes. Then to get off, I will lift the bar and you simply just stand up straight, and you will ski away from the chair to join your friends," I explained to Jerry, who nodded and was hanging on my every word.

"Ok," he acknowledged.

In front, Sid and quiet Alan were about to get off. Sid lifted the safety bar as the chair became level with the ground, they both stood up, quiet Alan successfully skied down the gentle slope to his waiting friends, while Sid got up at the same time with his bum-bag getting caught in the armrest of the chair, spinning him around like a rag doll to the turn area, and catapulting him headfirst into a pile of soft snow. This caused much laughter from the crowd watching.

Jerry saw the unfolding calamity in front of us, suddenly becoming panic-stricken and froze.

The level ground was fast approaching, I lifted the bar and told Jerry to stand up on the count of three.

"One… Two… Three!!"

I could see Jerry wasn't going to move. The choice was to stand now or sit there and go all the way back down the mountain. Only a split second to decide, I grabbed Jerry's coat and pulled him up into a standing position resulting in a perfect dismount.

We descended the gentle slope to join the rest of our group. Sid was still wriggling about in the pile of snow, cursing angrily in his effort to pull himself out. His hat was buried still and he goggles were sitting around his chin. His bum-bag was still attached to the chair lift disappearing back down the mountain.

We were all together at the top of the mountain enjoying the wonderful views. To the right-hand side was a 'nursery slope', ideal to teach the guys the basics, before heading down the mountain to the town below.

The guys received 'one to one' tuition all morning, and very soon, picked up the skills, mainly how to steer and stop, with much slipping, sliding and falling.

We paired up with our partners and slowly traversed our way down the mountain, stopping to regroup at regular intervals. Reg took the lead with Quiet Alan, and we all followed along an established track, keeping away from the fast runs, avoiding trees and crevasses.

The guys showed no fear and only had to be told commands once. They listened to our every word and stuck to their instructors like glue. We stayed in the routine for the next three days, building skills, speed and confidence. The lads were all a joy to teach.

Jerry and both Alans were keen to point their skis and fly down the mountain as fast as possible, unaware of dangers, especially small mounds of snow called 'Moguls', ideal for jumping. Quite often, the lads would end in a heap after encountering these dangers. Jumping moguls takes months of practise, as many people come unstuck on the landing resulting in broken bones.

Wednesday evening came round quickly. Excitement was high with the guys, as they had remembered it was disco night. All dressed up with wide lapel shirts and smart trousers, they were keen to get there.

The carers decided to stay back, treating it as an evening off. They probably wanted to hit the gluhwein again. They guys chose a meal from the hotel menu, without the normal routine of having to explain each dish. Sausage and chips all round.

After a short walk in the freezing night air, we arrived in the main square, with a central sculpture of an Austrian skier. In front of the sculpture was a large inn, wrapped with a queue of people waiting to go into the disco. Eventually, we entered a large dark dance hall, full of people younger than us, bopping around on the dance floor. Lights were flashing to the beat of the music in various bright colours. We set up camp at a large rectangular table, with long bench seats each side. Annie managed to find a chair for Reg, while Eddy and Sid came over to our table with two trays of drinks.

The Motley Crew disappeared into the dancing crowd, happily jigging about, causing much attention to the local teenage gangs. Dave kept checking in with us, sipping his Fanta. We could hear Noisy Alan over the music. The guys were buzzing with excitement as they were strutting their stuff off the dance floor.

There was a group of about ten young lads, I noticed when we came in, pointing and laughing at Reg's strange walk.

They claimed the table next to ours, drinking more, and more, becoming louder and ruder. They were all local, speaking Austrian, and aged in their late teens to early twenties. Eddy asked them politely to behave at one point, which fell on deaf ears. Eventually, they got bored and left, muttering abuse to us in their native tongue.

The guys joined us after a while for a much-needed drink, all sweating and enjoying themselves without a care in the world.

Around eleven o'clock we put on our coats, rounded everybody up, and left. The bitterly cold air snatched our breath as we went outside. Suddenly Annie and Sid had snowballs thrown at them, both hitting them in their faces. I was next to receive a direct hit, followed by the rest of us. We were ambushed by the bunch of lads who were taking the piss at the venue. Snowballs were smashing into us from all directions. Reg was hit in his neck, making him lose balance, slipping on the icy pavement, flat on his face, with his legs tangled beneath him. Annie went to his rescue and pulled him into a nearby bar, where the bar staff managed to get him back on his tin legs.

Eddy and Sid's Army training kicked in, both shouting.

"Come on boys. Let's get them." Nothing like the battles in Afghanistan, I thought.

We all grabbed chunks of snow and moulded them into snowballs, and launched them at our attackers. The Motley Crew held back, with all five of them picking up slabs of ice that had formed under the roof of a nearby building. I could see the lads hurling these slabs of ice with surprising accuracy, falling hard onto their targets. Screams were coming from some of these bullies. The crew carried on firing these blocks of ice, some disc-shaped, skimming across the road like pebbles in a pond. The guys had no fear and seemed to enjoy every moment of this added adventure.

Annie patched up Reg's cut chin and joined us in the ambush. Meanwhile, the battle had been won, with a hasty retreat of our attackers, following a heavy rain of ice hitting them. Noisy Alan and Dave were incredibly strong, showing no fear at all. They even went as close as they could to propel their missiles onto the targets.

A short stroll back to the hotel listening to the crew going over their adventure in every detail made us all smile. Reg was limping awkwardly on his metal legs, whilst holding a scarf up to his cut chin. The carers were waiting at the bar, surrounded by empty bottles and glasses. Noisy Alan couldn't wait to tell them of our evening out. Reg flopped onto a comfy chesterfield while Annie patched him up properly with some of the contents of her first aid box. Reg had noticed that one of his legs had twisted out of shape slightly, due to his heavy fall.

We retired for the night to catch some sleep, ready for another busy day.

The next few days went well, despite a heavy snowstorm, forcing us to take shelter in a mountainside cafe, where we had a welcoming hot goulash soup, fries and hot chocolate. Unfortunately, the crew didn't put their skis in the rack provided, they just dumped them in a heap right in front of the door. The manager, angrily came up to our table, already annoyed with the noisy banter coming from the guys.

"What's is wrong with you. Why do you block the door with your skis? Are you simple?" he said in perfect English.

As he was blasting us for a silly mistake, the crew turned to him, clearly embarrassed at being told off, and smiled at him. He realised what he had said and walked away.

We finished our hot chocolate, and Sid was happy for us to carry on, during the break in the storm. As we left the cafe, the manager apologised to us and shook our hands. He offered us his speciality sausages when we go back next time.

The next day, the conditions were perfect. The storm had blown over leaving powdery snow behind. We all arrived at the top of the mountain, checked our equipment ready for a fast descent for the first time using a quicker route. We buddied up to our partners, making sure everyone was ready and happy.

Reg collapsed to the floor knocking Freddie over in the process. Annie and I quickly got to him, thinking he had a heart attack or worse.

"The bloody support strap has broken on my legs. I won't be able to stand!" he moaned.

We were relieved that is wasn't anything more serious, however, we now had a problem. How do we get him down the mountain? Our plan was to get Reg to the ski hire shop to borrow some tools from the miserable manager and get Reg back on his feet.

Reg asked us to help him remove the legs completely, so we wedged him up to Annie's rucksack and unclipped the legs. Sid made several suggestions, as a crowd was gathering, amazed at the strange situation.

"We either get the snowcat up here to rescue you and take you back down the mountain, or ride pillion on the skibob and slowly traverse down? What would you prefer?"

Reg answered, "I'll go pillion. It will be quicker. Who is the lightest to ride with?"

The ideal driver would be Eddy, as he was a motorcycle stunt rider anyway, but he was two stone heavier than me. It was decided that I drive the skibob down with Reg on the back, with his false legs strapped to the handlebars.

We got onto the skibob, Reg gripping on to the rear saddle bar with one hand, and his other hand across my chest. Eddy took my skis and Annie took Reg's heavy boots. I fitted Reg's foot skis to my boots making it possible to steer. The rest of the party left having a good head start.

The crowd were watching us, some even filming us with their video cameras, as we inched forward to the slope leading to the main downward run.

My intention was to traverse slowly, back and forth until we reach the bottom. We were off. The skibob strained under the weight as we cut through the snow. It was difficult to manoeuvre, as it was like riding a bike with skis instead of wheels, with a bag of potatoes on my back. We were very top-heavy, gathering much-unwanted speed. Reg was gripping tighter, only holding his body in place by the strength of his arms. We managed two traverses. I could see the rest of our group like dots in the distance, making good progress. People were skiing past us, although we were now travelling at a much faster pace.

I turned, leaning right to make the next traverse, when one of the legs dislodged, jamming the handlebar mechanism. The handlebars were now wedged in a straight forward position. No matter how hard I bashed and tugged, it wouldn't release. We slipped away from the traverse line and headed straight down the mountain. I knew we were now in trouble. We were going far too fast to lay the bob down and crash. My only choice was to hang on and wait to get to the bottom, where the gradient will become shallow.

"Hang on Reg!!" I shouted. Reg also knew we were in a mess.

"Don't worry we will be fine!" he replied.

I had no choice, but to keep the line and hang on. A normal ski down this mountain would take forty-five minutes. We are going to do it in five minutes at this speed, if we make it.

Suddenly we hit a steep gradient, surrounded by moguls. The next second we were in the air on the start of a mogul jump. We hit the second mogul, launching us about six foot in the air, then another with the same result. This went on for about seven times. I was amazed we were still upright. My chest and shoulder were in pain with the pressure of Reg's weight hanging on to me. The bottom of the mountain was now in sight, also, the concrete base of the chair lift pylon was right in our path too. I desperately tried to slow down with my feet, without success, losing both foot skis in the process. Within seconds the concrete was gaining on us. I knew if we hit it, we wouldn't survive.

I couldn't steer at all now, and to make matters worse, the bob frame had cracked after jumping the moguls a few seconds ago.

I shouted to Reg. "Prepare to dump it. I'm going to lean left on three..."

Reg released his tight grip on me and shouted back. "Ok... go for it."

"One ... Two ... Three!" I shouted, both leaning left at the same time.

The handlebars and Reg's legs dug into the snow and catapulted us into a three hundred and sixty-degree spin. A combined weight of twenty-three stone was launched back into the air with the bob now split into two pieces. I landed hard and bounced back into the air again. Reg's torso gripped snow and began to roll past me like a bowling ball. He ended up as large snowball, eventually slowing him down. I was gathering snow all around me, with a huge cloud flicking up behind. The concrete base was now metres away, as we slowed down to a stop. The crowd below were watching the impending disaster unfold, and clapped when we eventually came to a stop.

Sid, Eddy and Annie ran towards us, unsure what state they would find us in. Reg was lying in a ball of snow, trying to move. I laid still, as a cloud of snow dust settled around me. We were both shocked, but surprisingly not hurt. I sat up and looked over to the crowd of people, and saw the crew and their carers standing watching with disbelief that we were ok. Some of them were crying.

Annie checked us over while Eddy collected all the broken pieces of the skibob and Reg's twisted legs. Sid scooped up the broken foot skis and our hats and goggles. We were offered a sledge by a kind family to pull Reg back into town.

The miserable hire shop manager reluctantly lent us his workshop to be able to repair Reg's legs. A strange request especially as he was already livid with us for breaking the ski bob…

It took Eddy and I all afternoon to repair the strapping points on the metal legs, and reset the connecting arms. Reg reattached his legs and commented that they were better than before. After an eventful morning, we decided to go back to the hotel for a rest, and a few beers.

Back at the hotel, about thirty local Austrians were having their weekly bridge game in the dining room, huddled around further tables set up in the reception area.

They were all elderly, sitting around tables in silence, drinking tea. The silence was broken as we all walked in with our skis and boots. The reception lady shushed us, putting her finger to her mouth.

The doors banged behind us, as we rattled our way in, with noisy Alan on top form. I could see the locals turning to us, looking daggers for disturbing their peace. Unfortunately, we had to walk past them to get to the boot room. Noisy Alan noticed that they were playing cards and shouted, "SNAP!" The other guys followed suit. Clause came running out of his office, waving his arms about telling us off.

The carers decided to take the guys swimming for a couple of hours while we rested and sat by the log fire. Eddy and Annie went off into the town to buy some awards to give out on the last evening. Reg hobbled in with an annoying squeak coming from the newly fitted straps, apologising to every bridge player as he past them.

The distant sound of noisy Alan came to our ears. All the guys were in the lift, heading for their rooms to get changed after their swim. The carers were using the dressing rooms by the pool. It appeared that the guys had escaped to do their own thing. The lift door opened to reveal the Motley Crew giggling and having fun, suddenly as the lift door was closing, Jerry was pushed out completely naked into the reception area as the Alan's ripped the towel from him. The lift doors shut, leaving Jerry standing there pushing all the buttons to retrieve the lift.

The bridge players looked in horror at the sight of Jerry's naked body wandering around the reception area. Sid got up and went over to him covering him up with his jacket. Hoots of laughter came from the lift. The ordeal was over for Jerry when the lift returned a minute later.

We found out that Jerry had put talcum powder in both Alans boots, so when they put them on, they would get a face full of white powder. Revenge is a dish best served cold.

The last two days went quickly, ending in a prize-giving on the last evening. Clause had kindly arranged to ask his friend, the town's Mayor to give out the awards. They were delighted to all receive an award and certificate. There was a 'Mutley Award' for Reg and me for braking a bob and having the most spectacular crash.

Eddy and I loaded all the cases into the coach and everyone sat down ready for the long journey to Munich Airport. As we departed the town, the guys noticed the group of lads that ambushed us after the disco. They were putting their tongues out and sticking their fingers up at them. Jerry even tried to do a moonie at them, was stopped by Cheryl. "I think people have seen a bit too much of your bum this week," she snapped.

We all had the same flight back to Stanstead. The customs area was a bit of a nightmare with the guys squabbling over passports, however we got through and waited for Reg. The alarms kept becoming activated as Reg went through, because his metal legs set them off. We said our goodbyes, with the guys not wanting to go, so we promised to do this again in the future. We did try and plan another ski trip, but, unfortunately, events took over with three of the instructors unable to commit. The tragic terrorist attack on 9/11 put a stop to our plans the following year.

The year later, Annie rang me, to tell me that Eddy died in a tragic motorbike accident. Noisy Alan lost both his parents within a few months of each other, resulting in him refusing to eat, and becoming ill. Alan died of a broken heart shortly after.

Reg wanted me to join him with the remainder of the group in 2002.

Eleven

There were always clients coming in and out of the office, especially during the Spring and Summer months. Sometimes it was impossible to remember all their names, so we invented nicknames for some of them.

There was confusion when we were dealing with two Mrs Browns. We called one of them Jimmy Cranky because she was a small lady with short cropped ginger hair. The other we called 'Mrs Silly Voice of the Year Winner', because she had the most peculiar annoying voice. This sort of banter between the staff, often happens in most office environments, it is harmless, and just a bit of fun. However, the confusion over the 'Mrs Browns' was highlighted when one of them rang the office to be answered by Carly. "Bill. Silly voice of the year for you on line two," she said.

I had no idea that the call hadn't been put on hold, with Mrs Brown hearing all Carly's remarks.

I picked up the call. "Good morning, Mrs Brown, how are you today?"

She replied, "Hello. Yes, I'm fine thank you. Just a bit confused with your receptionist. She said something about a silly voice."

I was quiet for a few seconds, processing this information, and realising what had just happened, I replied. "Oh yes, she was talking to some children in the office at the same time as picking up your call, and must have got into a muddle."

Carly looked mortified, going bright red and putting her hand across her mouth.

"Oh, I see… It's just my Grandchildren are always calling me Granny funny voice, so I'm quite used to it, you see," she stated.

I managed to sidetrack the conversation, thinking I got away with it this time.

A similar incident happened soon after when another client came into the office to provide proof of identification. Lucas was dealing with him during a quiet and calm office atmosphere.

Mr Bell had given Lucas his driving license and passport to photocopy. Lucas took these documents to Mary's office to photocopy them, at the back of the building. We could all hear their conversation coming from Mary's office. To my horror, I could hear Lucas's loud voice. "Hey… this guy's called Dennis Donald Bell… can you believe it? Ding Dong Bell…" Followed by silly sniggering.

I tried to distract Mr Bell from the voices coming from the back. He sat down at my desk and said. "Don't worry son. My parents must have hated me, giving me that name… still, it could have been worse."

"How do you mean?" I asked, feeling a bit stupid.

He replied, "I was in the Army with a guy called 'Private Parts'… So I got away lightly." We both laughed, especially when Lucas appeared and realised what had happened, saying. "Well, I was called Shrek at school because I was six foot tall when I was twelve."

"And ugly," Mr Bell said.

We all laughed, and when Mr Bell rang the office in future, he introduced himself as 'Ding Dong'.

The following weekend started with a thunderstorm, with constant rain. Terry had been dealing with the owner of a small terraced house in Westcliff. His name was Mr Thwaite, and over time, after getting to know him, he was known as Mr Twat.

Mary said, "Mr Twat on line one."

"Not again. What could he possibly want now?" he gasped, picking up the phone.

"Hello again Mr Twa… Thwaite. How can I help you?"

This had been the third phone call in forty minutes. It was clear that some clients were impossible to please, no matter how far you bend over backwards for them. Mr Twat complained that his property details were not up to his exacting, pernickety standard, and wanted the full attention of anybody that took his call. It seemed that Mr Twat's standard would be impossible to reach.

"I want you to come back and take fresh photos, as the daffodils have died off, and I want the details to follow the seasons," Mr Twat demanded.

"Well it's pouring with rain at the moment, so today won't be a good idea," Terry explained.

After a few minutes of back and forth conversation, it was agreed that one of the staff would go back at ten in the morning when the sun would be at the right angle.

I went to take the new photos, as Terry was fed up with pandering to the vendor's changing whims. As I fiddled with the camera to improve the focus, out came Mr Thwaite shouting.

"No, no, no… stand nearer and take it from the left angle. Don't get the bins in. Then you can do the back garden."

I followed instructions, clicking away at the vendor's delight. He had my full attention and demanded more. "Stand here, go over there, don't get the satellite dish in focus and take one of the vegetable plot."

What should have been a quick 'drive-by' photo of the front of the property, turned into a mammoth photoshoot, taking over an hour. I managed to prize myself away, with Mr Thwaite following me to the car and still talking as I was driving away.

New details were prepared and sent to Mr Thwaite. After, Carly spent nearly a whole day copying and pasting the new photos onto the glossy brochures.

As expected, Mr Thwaite rang as soon as he received the amended brochure. A list of complaints poured over Carly's ears almost bringing her to tears. The complaints were totally unjust. "You have got the satellite dish in the photo. Can't you airbrush it out?" he moaned.

It was arranged that he comes into the office to discuss his complaints with me or Terry when we were back in. He couldn't wait and just turned up, waiting to speak to one of us. We both arrived at the office together, and saw Mr Twat clutching his details, marked with red ink in the areas that needed attention.

"Now look here, the text is all wrong, also the house looks too small in the photos," he said angrily.

"I am not changing it again. It is what it is, a small terraced house, not Buckingham Palace. Either take it or leave it! In other words, Mr Thwaite, if you can't accept these details, I suggest you take your business elsewhere. You have taken up far too much of our time, and secondly, I don't like the way you talk to the staff. I can only imagine what a pain in the arse you will be if we actually find you a buyer!" Terry ranted.

Mr Thwaite looked stunned at Terry's response. There was an awkward silence as he composed himself for a reply.

"How dare you speak to me like that. I have a good mind to report you," he retorted.

Terry was quick on his reply. "Who to? The 'Irritating Vendor Society', because you would win that with flying colours."

Mr Thwaite was so cross, he got up quickly out of his chair and lunged forward to punch Terry, who dodged out of the way.

"You try that again and I'll have you thrown out!" Terry said.

"I would like to see you try it sunshine, you just try!" he replied, clenching his fists, ready for another blow.

Terry replied. "I don't need to, as Lulu's here!"

"What do you mean Lulu's here, you ignorant sod?" he shouted.

Right on cue, a huge Shrek-like figure, all six foot and twenty stone, appeared into the office from around the back. Terry pointed saying. "That's Lulu."

Mr Twat turned around, seeing the hulking figure walking towards him, with hands the size of boxing gloves.

"I'm Lulu. And you're leaving now!" he said.

Mr Thwaite complained. "This is intimidation!"

Lulu picked up the wriggling vendor by his belt and threw him out the door onto the pavement, whilst saying, "Clear off and be intimidated elsewhere, and don't come back, Mr Twat!"

It appeared that Mr Thwaite tried the services of other agents over the next months, ending up being blacklisted from them as well.

I noticed a homemade for-sale board outside Mr Thwaite's house when I drove past. Who will he complain to now?

Things changed within both branches over the twenty-five years I worked with this company. Dawn, the receptionist at the other office, left to get married and became, Dawn Biddulph Pinchard. It seemed ironic that she ended up with a double-barrelled name, as when I first met her, she had not heard of hyphenated names.

Martin left the business and became a Surveyor. His Mohican haircut was just a funny memory. He often came into the office to collect keys and I always mentioned to him. "Make sure you notice whether the property is detached or semi-detached."

"Yeah, and I won't kick the dog too… ha ha!" he would say.

Stuart retired, and moved to the Spanish coast, working for 'H', looking after his yacht. He would sometimes pop in to see us when he was back in the UK, still wearing his 'second-hand car salesman's coat', and smoking roll-ups.

Graham left to start a lettings company with a Surveyor friend of his, maximising a rising market.

Twelve

I answered a phone call from a prospective viewer, trying to make an appointment to see 'Jokers Wild'. I recognised the voice at the other end of the phone, with my heart sinking as it was the unmistakable Mr Wong.

"Aww… Ello Mr Estate Agent Man… Remember me?" he said.

My memory of Mr Wong and his family was not a good pleasant one, as they trashed a house a few years ago, leaving me with hefty repair and cleaning bills. Surely this can't be the same Mr Wong? I thought, but it was. At least his children would have grown up now and will know how to behave.

"Yes, I do remember you, Mr Wong. When would you like to see 'Jokers Wild'?" I asked.

"I want to go Saturday at eleven if possible?" he asked.

Mr and Mrs Black went out for the day and left me a key to do the viewing. I arrived at the house, opened up and activated the fountain, with a burst of spluttering water cascading into the air, as Mr Black requested.

The house was spotless as usual with every detail staged for this viewing. The garden had been manicured within an inch of its life. This property had been on and off the market for many years, with continual improvements being made, to include a full-width Orangery, recently built.

The vendors had been extremely patient, however, being property developers knew the current market situation.

A bright 'Kermit-green' people carrier pulled up on the gravel drive, turning into a bay in front of the garage, spraying gravel onto the lawn. I was extremely glad Mr Black wasn't there to see that.

The occupants got out. "Ello, Mr Estate Agent man! Remember me? I am Mr Wong and this is my family," he said grinning.

"Hello, Mr Wong. I do remember you," I said. I was thinking, 'How could I forget you?'

His family, consisting of Mrs Wong and their three children, mostly teenagers, were all chattering excitedly in Chinese. I was worried about what damage they could do in this outstanding property, especially as the vendor is very fussy and has a short fuse.

I opened the massive panelled front door and followed them all in. I tried to keep them herded all together, as best as I could and asked them to take their shoes off. They respectfully followed me into every room, falling in love with the fine features of this wonderful house.

Mr Wong was happy to tell me all about how he could afford a house like this. Whilst we were exploring the vast amount of space inside, he was telling me that he inherited a large amount of money from his parents, who sold a printing company during the trade boom in the Eighties.

The children were far better behaved than my last encounter with them, which was a huge relief. The viewing seemed to go well without any problem. Forty minutes later the Wongs headed out of the house towards their car. "Vewy nice pwoperty, Mr Estate Agent man, like it vewy much. Will be in touch," he said, shaking my hand.

He did keep in touch, and surprisingly, the next day he made a full asking price offer and proceeded to exchange contracts. This was a real landmark victory for our office, to sell one of the most desirable houses in this part of Essex. Dealing with two very different personalities also presented its own problems, as both could be difficult and stubborn during the negotiations.

We decided to celebrate this success, so, in keeping with the Chinese theme, we went to a lovely Chinese restaurant recommended to us.

As we entered the restaurant, a friendly Chinese waiter ushered us to a large round table, three ladies, akin to Dame Edna, Lilly Savage and Danny La Rue. It was Claire and two of her cross-dressing friends, having a night out. Claire saw me and called out for my attention. We were introduced to her friends, both obviously men, badly dressed as women, with smudged makeup, crooked wigs and deep voices. This was turning into quite a surreal experience but provided some fun entertainment.

After a while, the three 'Women' pulled up their chairs to our table, creating quite a commotion, with shoes clacking on the marble floor, and the scrapping of heavy chairs being dragged over. They bickered with each other decided who was going to sit next to who.

We settled around a large round table, enjoying a vast variety of dishes.

"Aww … Ello Mr Estate Agent man."

I looked up and saw Mr Wong. I was surprised to see him, especially under the circumstances, that we were only here to celebrate his purchase of 'Jokers Wild'.

Handshakes all round with Mr Wong. "I own this restaurant, I hope you like the food?" he stated.

I had no idea that he was the owner of this restaurant. I replied, "Yes, very nice food, Lovely place and nice to see you too."

He politely left us to our meal, looking strangely at Claire and her friends.

We waited ages for the bill, then Mr Wong came over with a tray of drinks for us and said, "No charge for you. I am very pleased with my new house, and is my way to say thank you for help."

Even the three strange 'women' were included, although they gate-crashed our party. Amazingly we all had a great evening and seemed to be a hit with Mr Wong.

Over the following years, the Wongs bought two apartments for their older children.

I often drive past 'Jokers Wild' and think of the adventure of how it eventually sold.

The next day, I was invited by Rob Harrington, to accompany him to Manchester to see a dockside development he was involved in building.

Rob is a very successful property developer, specialising in large warehouse conversions adjacent to waterway within growing towns and cities.

His success was well known in the Estate Agency world, having recently finished a huge apartment block in Southend. Rob was an eccentric character, that I have been involved with since his first project ten years ago. His younger years he taught people to fly Helicopters in Australia before he became a property developer. He still dashes about the country in his pride and joy, a Robinson R44, complete with his company logo printed on both doors.

We had an early start, meeting at Southend Airport where his Helicopter was waiting. The weather was overcast, the forecast was for mild fog later in the day. I was glad to be flown to Manchester as the drive would have been a long haul.

Flight checks took about half an hour. Finally, we strapped ourselves in and waited for clearance to take off. Clearance came through on our headphones, and with a flick of some switches, we were off, reaching a height of three-thousand feet within minutes. Rob spoke all the time through the onboard microphone system, telling me of each manoeuvre, also pointing out familiar landmarks on the way. Although I felt very safe during the flight, it was extremely noisy and bumpy, especially when hit by a flank wind.

The weather became more overcast towards the north of the country, although the sun did try and break through as we approached Manchester. The arrangement with air traffic control was to land in a waste area, adjacent to Rob's building site, giving us a three-hour gap to inspect the site and then to fly back taking the same route.

A long cold tour of the luxury apartments and harbour area led to a welcoming coffee in a site office overlooking the waterfront. The point of this trip was to show me that this development would be almost identical to a project due to be started in the Summer, in a London dock area.

I gave Rob as much input as I could at this stage, excited with the promise of marketing around fifty new apartments overlooking the Thames, with a small harbour adjacent to a quaint commercial site, ideal for restaurant use.

The day was coming to an end, so we walked back to the Helicopter, noticing that the weather was closing in, prompting a quick flight check and clearance to take off from nearby Manchester Airport.

At eight hundred feet the visibility became very poor, as the fog had thickened, making the onward flight impossible. We dropped to three hundred feet and followed the M6 motorway for several miles. The crawling traffic's fog lights below became an important factor in our intention to land safely, without causing an accident. The fog thickened in cloudy patches. Rob's normal banter turned to dialogue with air traffic control at Manchester, desperately waiting for instructions to land. We were too far from Manchester Airport to be able to turn around, finding our only option was to land wherever was deemed to be safe, and away from built-up areas.

I was at this time getting nervous, however, I knew I was in safe hands. We descended to eighty feet and saw lights and what seemed to be a car parking area, possibly providing a safe place to land. I noticed the familiar 'golden arches' to a MacDonald's as we approached to land.

Rob said in his usual casual manner. "Fancy a Big Mac and fries?"

Before I had time to reply, we were hovering over the car park, scanning for a wide area to land. Within a few seconds, we were parked next to families, sitting in their cars enjoying their meals.

Small children were pointing excitedly, to see the sight of a helicopter parking next to them. People got out of their cars and crowded around to see what was going on, some taking photos, whilst Rob spoke to air traffic control, stated our position, stressing this was an emergency landing, then, suggested we make the most of it and grab a burger.

It seemed very weird going to a MacDonald's by helicopter, however, we decided to sit in the restaurant and wait for the fog to clear. As we were tucking into our burgers, it was clear we could be stranded for an hour at least. A Police car pulled up outside, with two officers getting out and slowly walking over to the Aircraft. One was talking on his radio, the other was putting 'Police aware' tapes around the cab of the Helicopter.

The people in the car park soon directed the officers to our table. We tried to explain our position, with a crowd watching and listening in.

We were arrested and taken to the nearest Police station, leaving an officer with the aircraft. The fog seemed to be clearing, which annoyed Rob because we could have been well on our way back. The Police did their checks with Manchester Airport and eventually became satisfied that we were not drug dealers or similar. An hour now wasted at the Police station, followed by a lift back to Macdonald's car park to find a cheering crowd and press photographers.

Rob finished the flight checks and started the rotors. Clearance came quickly as I think that Manchester Airport wanted us out the way as soon as possible. We took off to a sound of applause and continued on our journey.

The whole escapade was on the ten o'clock news according to friends and family.

Thirteen

I received a phone call from Reg asking me if I would like to join him at Buckingham Palace, as he had been chosen to receive a Knighthood for his services to charity over the years.

This was well deserved, and of course, I would be delighted to go as his guest along with Annie, whom he also invited.

It appeared that Reg didn't have any family members that he could ask. Annie went with him when he was honoured with a 'Military Cross' for bravery in active service from the Queen. Reg at that time was in a wheelchair, waiting for false legs to be made for him. I didn't know about this, as Reg was such a modest man, hardly ever speaking about his military history, especially the fact that he saved many of his colleagues lives by putting his life before theirs, losing both his legs from the hips down in the process.

Annie and I agreed to meet him outside the Palace. Arriving in plenty of time, waiting patiently in our best attire. Many people were arriving and congregating around the designated meeting place. We heard the distant clanking from a nearby drop off point, where we saw the familiar smiling figure staggering towards us. It was great to see him again especially on a memorable day like this.

We queued alongside many other smartly dressed people, buzzing with excitement for the day ahead.

After a short wait, a well-groomed Royal dignitary greeted us and ushered us to an opulent room with gilt-framed portraits of Royal Family members surrounding the grand décor on the walls. The Royal Aide spoke of the protocol and etiquette expected during the ceremony.

We were then taken into a large banqueting room aligned by rows of seats on a highly polished floor, leading to a raised area where Prince William would conduct the ceremony. In front of the raised area was a small run of a red carpet.

Classical music echoed softly around the grand hall as we were ushered to our designated seats. Most people were from military, medical or political backgrounds with a splattering of a few familiar faces from the film and television industry. Rod Stewart sat two rows in front of us, with his wife, looking very smart, although smaller than expected.

Prince William appeared with several of his staff and a spokesperson dressed in regal gowns, taking centre stage. The process started with many people receiving their honours before Reg from Prince William.

We sat quite near the back, waiting with anticipation for Reg's name to be called. Each recipient had to wait for their full name to be called, then walk towards the red carpet along the highly polished Canadian Pine floor and kneel to be knighted. Prince William would chat for about one minute to each person receiving their honour, then the recipient would walk backwards three paces before returning to their seat.

"Reginald Artimus Meadon" was called. Reg got up and clanked his way awkwardly along the shining floor in his new mirror polished shoes.

As Reg slowly approached the red carpet, suddenly within a split second, his legs went in different directions, as his shoes lost grip. His face dived the floor with a heavy thud. Unable to move his legs as an able-bodied person could, he clattered around to a sitting position with his legs almost in the splits position.

The whole calamity echoed loudly around the vast room, overwhelmed by Reg shouting, "Bollocks…"

Annie and I rushed to his aid, skidding along the floor. Two Royal Aides also came to his rescue, pulling him up to a vertical position. He regained balance quite quickly still cursing under his breath. Reg composed himself and continued gingerly towards the red carpet to be greeted by a smiling Prince William.

You could hear a pin drop whilst this drama unfolded, highlighting the bad language coming from Reg. His legs clanked loudly as he came to a halt on the red carpet, where he stood lopsided to shake hands with the Prince.

Reg was knighted whilst standing, then said to Prince William. "I am most terribly sorry that I swore when I took a tumble back there."

Prince William replied whilst shaking his hand again with both of his hands. "Don't worry. You should hear my Dad's foul language when he takes a tumble over one of the Corgis… the bastard things."

They chatted for at least five minutes, much longer than anyone else during the whole process. Reg shuffled back three paces as the Royal Aides had instructed, then with a wobble, he turned to negotiate the polished floor. His legs slowly moved in the correct direction as Annie and I flanked him towards his seat.

Reg mentioned on the way out that his favourite prize was the 'Mutley Award' he received in Austria.

The next day led me to value a bungalow called 'Enterprise', owned by James Kirk.

This was a strange experience, as the bungalow was not what it seemed. The owner had changed his name by deed poll many years ago. I remember selling him the bungalow when it was a probate sale, noting that he was a bit odd then.

I could see when I pulled up outside that the bungalow looked quite ordinary from the outside, apart from being painted in battleship grey, with numerous lights set into the soffit boards and pathways.

The front door was made of metal with a circular porthole, inset with smoked glass. James Kirk answered the door in full star trek uniform, inviting me into his spaceship, as he called it.

I realised that this chap was obviously a huge 'Star Trek' fan, living his private life as Captain James Kirk, he actually had a real resemblance to the actor, William Shatner.

The bungalow had been totally gutted with all internal walls taken out, apart from a bedroom and bathroom wall. The walls were covered in hundreds of dials and twinkling lights, with false windows looking onto planets and stars. The floor was an industrial type metal with a central raised area housing two large leather office-style chairs, each with a dashboard wrapping around them with a joystick in front.

It was like walking around a film set, an exact copy of the Starship Enterprise. Thousands of pounds must have been spent to make this possible, even the noises coming from the many computer panels were the same as I remember from the TV series. I pushed a button next to the bedroom door, and as in the series, the doors opened automatically making the swooshing noise followed by a beep. The bedroom was lined in stainless steel, with porthole windows and a bed that folded out from a purpose-made section in the wall.

The bathroom was the only room that looked normal, with no 'Trekky' modifications.

The rear garden was mainly a courtyard but remodelled to look like an aircraft wing, surrounded by six-foot black painted fence panels, with many small lights cleverly inset into areas to look like stars at night. There was also a type of black netting covering the whole area, making it very dark. In the corner was a 'Klingon' made from fibreglass, down-lit in a green light.

This was a property that kept on giving with so much to look at and try to understand. James Kirk proudly showed off every aspect of his Enterprise, having admitted that he may have gone way over the top with the 'spaceship' renovations.

I had the problem of trying to figure out a price for it, bearing in mind there would be hardly any market for this type of renovation, unless we were lucky enough to find another 'Trekky' as a buyer.

I presented James Kirk with a price that I thought a potential buyer may pay, bearing in mind that most people would want to restore it back to a two bedroomed bungalow.

James Kirk told me that he worked for the Tax office and may be moved to Milton Keynes, so there was a real possibility that he may have to take his spaceship to another county. He seemed pleased with the valuation and sent me on my way saying, "May the force be with you."

Ironically, I was due to complete my Tax return and thought of my client.

A young negotiator came into the office to collect a key, he introduced himself, then said that he knew us when he was about nine or ten. He was the young lad we called 'Kung Fu Kid', and proudly mentioned to Terry in front of all the staff. "Do you remember me, I was about nine when I kicked you in the nuts?"

"Yes. I remember you, I right little sod, I cringe every time I drive past your old house," Terry said with a smile.

My world came to an abrupt end, as my increasing lower back pain landed me in hospital, being unable to walk, with the added problem of pneumonia. Several scans and blood tests ended in a long stay in a cancer ward.

Proffessor Ian Jones sat next to me and explained that I have Multiple Myeloma, a cancer of the bone marrow. My chances of survival were very slim, unless I have a bone marrow transplant within the next six months. There was no time to find a suitable donor, so the plan was to use my own stem cells as soon as I finished six months of chemotherapy.

The cancer had already spread to my spine, presenting more problems. Before starting the gruelling course of chemotherapy I was taken to have Radiotherapy on my T7 vertebrae, a quick process, with little pain.

Over the next six months, I was kept in a private room with limited visits from the outside world, mainly because my immune system had collapsed, and that I wasn't up to seeing anybody. I struck up a good rapport with Ian Jones, finding him to be a brilliant specialist in curing cancers and a genuinely nice person. The nurses called him 'Indiana Jones' as he looked a bit like Harrison Ford, and also a play on his name. He was also interested in a property, planning to move to a larger house within the next year or so. He gave me hope in saying that when I am better, my aim would be to find him and his family a suitable house.

I asked him. "What would be the ideal house to buy?" To my surprise, he replied, "Jokers Wild". Have you heard of it?"

"Yes. I sold several years ago to a Chinese family," I replied.

"Well, that is a coincidence. My friend lives next door, he is a heart surgeon. Also, he is my golfing partner, so I see the house when I pick him up for our game," he explained.

I promised that if 'Jokers Wild' came onto the market I would let him know first.

My condition worsened, causing me to be taken to St Bart's Hospital, in London to start the transplant procedure. Every week, Indiana came to my room to explain the medical journey I started, every step of the way, and the ongoing process.

At this stage, I had no idea whether I would survive, especially as people on the same ward as me, often younger and fitter didn't make it.

The thought of leaving my children was not an option, I had to survive no matter what. Indiana kept telling me, at every opportunity, that I have to get through this and get back to work, so I can find him a house.

I know he was just giving me the confidence to get through this, however, it worked.

Six weeks after my stem cell transplant my platelets were edging upwards, eventually to the satisfaction of Indiana, and the team to be able to go home.

Three months later I was back at work, full time, and only too pleased to be involved with normal life again.

I had forgotten how demanding the job can be, but nothing as bad as being in hospital. My outlook on life changed tremendously, not taking life too seriously, and certainly not taking any rudeness from clients.

A year went by very quickly, as it took that time to get used to the property market again, also becoming acquainted with property prices in a quickly moving market. Clients that I dealt with twenty years ago were coming back for another move, or for their children buying their first property.

It was refreshing to see Kevin walking past our door in the morning with a new Great Dane, as Scooby passed away, leaving Kevin very low and lonely. He was normally keen to chat, especially when he lost Scooby.

The new Great Dane, called Scooby Two, was even bigger and stronger, dragging Kevin along with very little notice of instructions.

Fourteen

My Dad was now ninety-three, having been blind for nearly thirty years and now suffering from dementia. He had been in a fantastic nursing home for four years enjoying the best possible care, by a team of wonderful carers.

His nursing home was very local, giving me the peace of mind that family and friend could visit as often as possible.

The Dementia caught up with him, rendering him unable to eat. He went to Southend Hospital, into a private room where he quickly deteriorated with only a few hours to live. His family was by his side holding his hand when an Indian Doctor came in and asked us all politely to leave the room. I assumed that she was going to administer some medication, perhaps to make him more comfortable.

I watched through the small window to see what was happening and saw the Doctor leaning over towards Dad's ear, talking to him very closely, whilst stroking his hand. She spoke for at least ten minutes, which I thought was a bit odd, however, perhaps not unusual.

She then kissed his forehead, and with a tear in her eye, she walked out of the room. I noticed her NHS badge with her name, 'Doctor Prisha Khan'.

Dad passed away within a few minutes of the Doctor saying her goodbyes. It hadn't clicked in my brain that the Doctor was 'Prisha', the young Indian girl Dad sponsored through school and University over thirty-five years ago.

I didn't recognise her, as time had moved on, and she obviously didn't recognise me, however, when she left the room, she did hesitate for a split second, as if she wanted to stop and introduce herself.

My intention was to get back in touch with her and invite her to Dad's funeral. I left several messages, without success. When going through the paperwork in Dad's memory box, there were many letters from Prisha, explaining in great detail of her adventures after she qualified as a Doctor, there was even a wedding invite. I am not sure whether Dad replied by letter, however, he often mentioned that he had phoned her, happily sharing her progress with me. The letters stopped twenty years ago, possibly as Dad's eyesight had worsened to the point of total blindness.

I am sure he would have known that Prisha had spoken to him at the end of his life, hopefully feeling comfort from that.

I decided to get back to work and fill my mind with positivity, as the last two weeks had been very stressful.

It wasn't long to find a familiar voice at the end of the phone.

"Ello Mr Estate Agent man… remember me?"

Of course, I knew straight away that this was Mr Wong… How could I forget?

"Hello, Mr Wong. How are you?" I asked.

"I am not so good really," Mr Wong replied.

"I'm sorry to hear that. How can I help you?" I asked with concern in my voice.

"I need you to sell 'Jokers Wild'... can you come and see me?" he asked.

I punched the air excited with the prospect of selling 'Jokers Wild' again. Terry and Lulu watched and listened with interest to my conversation.

"Ok, it will be great to help you. When can I come and see you?" I asked.

"You come here tomorrow at ten o'clock, please. Don't forget your camera," he requested.

I was really pleased that he had come back to us to sell his house. A feather in our cap I thought, especially with the number of new Estate Agents that had opened up in the last few years.

The next day, I pulled up onto the gravel drive, parking where I had parked many times before over the years.

At first glance, nothing much had changed, apart from the swaying silver birch trees, standing taller like guards defending the boundaries, providing much-needed shade from the morning sun.

The fountain was in full flow, spurting jets of water high into the air, under-lit by bright coloured lights, changing sequence every few seconds.

I walked towards to newly painted, bright red front door, crunching across the gravel with every step. I knocked the gold dragons head door knocker, as Mr Wong opened the heavy door, to greet me with a huge smile.

He warmly shook my hand and introduced me to his wife, who I had met before, and remembered that she didn't speak any English.

Mr Wong looked different to when I saw him about five years ago, it was his teeth. He seemed to have a complete set of bright white implants, all a few sizes too big, impairing his ability to talk. He was difficult to understand anyway, because of his strong Chinese accent, now he was spitting as he spoke.

I followed him through to the massive reception hall, featuring two winding stairways leading up to a central gallery. The walls had inset sunken arches displaying ornate blue crackle glazed Chinese 'Dogs of Fo', proudly standing about four feet high, down lit with subtle blue lighting.

The inside of this property is so different from when the Blacks owned it. The walls are papered with hand-rolled bold red and gold paper, with Flamingos and other birds displaying bright colours.

Standing centrally in the reception hall is a terracotta elephant looking directly at the front door, as if it was guarding the entrance. I wondered how on earth they managed to get the elephant in, must have needed a forklift.

The interior continued to surprise me, like a present that keeps on giving. The décor was similar to an upmarket Chinese restaurant in Soho. The kitchen was the same as I remembered it, apart from the smell of Chinese cooking, and the many woks and pans hanging from a rack, like bats above the central island.

Mrs Wong offered me a cup of tea, whilst I was taking photos of the kitchen, I was pleased to accept.

I continued taking photos, as instructed by Mr Wong, in each room, capturing in great detail the many fine features.

Mr Wong took my tea into his study and invited me in to discuss his intentions and details of his oncoming move. He closed the door behind him, leaving Mrs Wong clattering about in her kitchen.

"You see… I don't want to sell, but have to sell," Mr Wong said showing much disappointment in his expression.

"Oh, I am sorry to hear that," I said, wiping the spit from my face from Mr Wong.

"We have got to sell … I am velly sad to let it go… velly, velly sad," Mr Wong said whilst pouring scented tea into small china cups.

I listened intently, wondering why they have to sell, knowing that they had the most successful Chinese restaurant in the area. They also bought their children properties, and they own this magnificent home, full of expensive furnishings.

Mr Wong explained almost in tears, "You see I owe much money… lots of money… so must pay debts… you see," looking down at the floor.

"Oh, I see…" I said, feeling quite sorry for him.

Mr Wong looked me straight in my eyes and said "You see my wife is big gambler… big gambler… she spent much money at casino… lots of debt… you see she much out of control. So we move in with my son and sell house to pay all debts."

We sipped our tea, settling on a price, and a suitable commission structure. Mr Wong seemed happier that he had put a plan into action.

Both Mr and Mrs Wong came out to the car with me, very grateful for the prompt service and the advice I had given them. The wind caught the jetting water from the fountain and sprayed a large cloud of ice-cold mist over all of us. I pushed the camera into the flap of my jacket to protect it as I didn't want to ruin another one.

Mr Wong put his head into my car, through the open window, explaining that the soaking from the fountain must be a sign from the Gods. As he was saying this, I was getting a soaking from Mr Wong's ill-fitting teeth.

Back at the office, the girls transformed my new photos onto a fabulous glossy brochure. There was a buzz of excitement about this instruction, however, I did promise to let my Consultant know if 'Jokers Wild' came onto the market.

I left a message on Ian Jones's answer machine at the hospital, and dropped off a brochure by hand to his office. A day went past with no contact, which I thought was strange, as at our monthly reviews to discuss my blood results, he always mentions the property market, and if any interesting properties had come on.

The next day the office door flew open and in burst Ian Jones. He came straight over to my desk smiling from ear to ear.

"Thank you for your message… I thought I would come and see you face to face. I would like to buy 'Jokers Wild'," he said.

I replied with hidden excitement, "Oh great… I will set it all up for you. Firstly, would you like to look around just to make sure you like the house?"

"Yes please, although it won't make much difference as I want to change the house to our taste anyway," he replied.

I set up a viewing for that afternoon. The Wong's were very pleased to show them around.

The next day Ian Jones confirmed that he wanted to buy the house and offered the full asking price and a firm completion date. The deal was done finding both parties delighted with the outcome. Mr Wong asked if Mr Jones would like to buy the elephant? Possibly worrying about how he was going to remove it.

The Jones's moved in with the elephant still standing proud guarding the front door.

Several weeks went by, with my monthly appointment due today. I went to meet Ian Jones at his office as I did every month to discuss my ongoing treatment, although we spoke more about 'Joker's Wild' than medical facts.

As I got up to go Ian Jones handed me a parcel wrapped in brown paper. "This is for you," he said.

"Go on, open it now," he said.

I tugged at the brown paper to discover a name plaque reading 'Jokers Wild'.

Ian explained, "I have changed the name of the house to 'INDIANA', and thought you might like the old name plaque?

I was delighted with this, as it would become a trophy, a way to remember this landmark house.

Acknowledgements

To Larry Keay for training me as an Estate Agent and for making my working life fun and interesting. Without him, there wouldn't be this book. Also for watching my back when I was having a bone marrow transplant and was in hospital for many months.

To my darling wife Jenny for believing in me, giving me unlimited support over the years. And to my two beautiful daughters, Nadia and Yasmin for giving me the reason to fight cancer and share a future together.

I would also like to thank Louis de Bernières for his encouragement and inspiration.

About William Downes

I was born in Newbury in 1961 and went to Park House School, then onto to study art at SEEVIC college in Thundersley. My first job was at Chinamend in Knightsbridge, restoring broken works of art, being commissioned by some members of the Royal Family, John Hurt and Ava Gardner. After becoming a shareholder, the company sold, leading me to join the Police Force. This was short-lived, so following my interest in property, I became an Estate Agent for the remainder of my working life.

After being diagnosed with Multiple Myeloma, months of chemotherapy followed, and a bone marrow transplant. Thankfully I made a good recovery and returned to work. The cancer returned, forcing me to retire early, and eventually start a quieter life in Norfolk.

I now paint and draw cartoons, always looking at the funny side of life. I enjoy time with my Grandchildren, sketching personalised cartoon books for them.

Available worldwide from Amazon

---

www.mtp.agency

www.facebook.com/mtp.agency

@mtp_agency